# How to Write Mysteries

## About the Author

S hannon OCork wrote three T. T. Baldwin mysteries, precursors to today's popular subgenre of novels with the female sleuth. *Sports Freak* and *End of the Line* were named to *The New York Times* Notable Books of the Season List. *Hell Bent for Heaven* was named one of the Ten Best Mysteries of 1983 by *Detroit News*. Her first bestseller was *Turning Point* and was followed by *Ice Fall* and *The Murder of Muriel Lake*. She is currently at work on a new novel titled *At Night They Purr*.

A native Kentuckian, Ms. OCork is active in Mystery Writers of America and married to MWA Grand Master, Hillary Waugh. The mystery-writing couple live in Guilford, Connecticut on Long Island Sound with their cat Mr. Boswell.

# HOW TO WRITE MYSTERIES

*by*
*Shannon OCork*

 Writer's Digest Books    *Cincinnati, Ohio*

93  92            5   4   3

**Library of Congress Cataloging-in-Publica-
tion Data**

OCork, Shannon.
    How to write mysteries/Shannon OCork.
        p. cm.
    Includes index.
    ISBN 0-89879-372-6
    1. Detective and mystery stories—Author-
ship.   I. Title.
PN3377.5.D4036      1989       89-34317
808.3'872—dc20                      CIP

*Designed by Carol Buchanan*

*To* **All of Us**

*Those who, wanting to write a Mystery, do or did or will . . .*

*Greetings, comrades!*

# Contents

## Introduction by
# Hillary Waugh

There is a saying that a good mystery writer can write a better straight
novel than most straight novelists can write a mystery. There is a lot
of truth to the claim, as a number of well-known novelists who have tried
their hand at a mystery can testify. Why is this so? What is there about
the mystery—which seems such a deceptively easy thing to write—that
makes it so difficult?

The reasons are two. The first is that the disciplines of the mystery
novel are also the requirements for good storytelling. The second is that
*that* is exactly what they are: *Disciplines*.

Too many storytellers, even good storytellers, ramble. They wander
away from the subject, they get involved with irrelevant minutiae, they
fall under the sway of their fancies. For this, in the straight novel, they
may be forgiven. But not in the mystery. The mystery is a tightly told
tale in which every action, every nuance, every shade of character must
contribute to the story. If it doesn't, it doesn't belong. In the mystery, no
digressing is allowed. No meandering. No flights of fancy. If the mystery
author wants to take a stand, promote a viewpoint, or rant against injus-
tice, he or she can only do so within the framework of the story. What he
says must move the story along for, in the mystery, it is the story that
matters. Why? Because the mystery novel is a game between author and
reader, the goal of which is Find the Villain, and Foul Play is not allowed.
The reader is entitled to expect that everything in the mystery relates to
that objective. This, then, lays a heavy stricture upon the mystery writer.
He may express himself as much as he wants, but he may only do so
within the framework of the mystery form—meaning it must have a bear-
ing on the plot. It must relate to Find the Villain. To work under such a
limitation requires artistry and skill. That is what makes the mystery such
a demanding art form. The mystery, to the novel, is what the sonnet is to
poetry.

Lest the would-be mystery writer become too easily discouraged by the
above, let it be pointed out that the rules that govern the mystery story are
not difficult to master. There are six, as follows:

1

1. All clues discovered by the detective must be made available to the reader. (That is where Fair Play comes in.)
2. The murderer must be introduced early. (This doesn't mean he must make a personal appearance, but the reader must know of his existence. Quite obviously, one should not introduce a new character on page 214 and reveal him as the villain on page 215.)
3. The crime must be significant. The reader's attention isn't going to be held by "who threw the overalls in Mrs. Murphy's chowder?" It is for significance that the crime is usually murder, though kidnapping, blackmail, theft, and the like will also do.
4. There must be detection. The solution mustn't be stumbled on, it must be sought and found.
5. The number of suspects must be known, and the murderer must be among them.
6. Nothing extraneous may be introduced. This is the "toughie" but it shouldn't be that hard a rule to follow if you remember the kind of story you're writing.

These are the rules that fence in the writer. How to work within these fences to produce a saleable book is what Shannon OCork will be discussing in the following pages.

But what about the mystery? Where did it come from and why does it intrigue as it does?

The mystery story began with Edgar Allan Poe and his "Murders in the Rue Morgue," followed by "The Mystery of Marie Roget." Here, for the first time, we have a tale, not just of crime, but of a detective solving that crime. That is the essence of the mystery story. There is a crime and an effort is made to solve that crime. That effort—detection—is what the mystery story is all about. (See rule 4 above.)

Poe not only introduced detection into fiction, he introduced the *memorable* detective. C. Auguste Dupin, who solves the murders in the Rue Morgue and the mystery of Marie Roget, not only amazes us by his deductive ability, he presents us with a unique life-style, living by night, sleeping by day, existing almost totally out of sight of the sun.

The theme of the memorable detective was picked up and elaborated upon a half-century later by Sir Arthur Conan Doyle whose Sherlock Holmes is not only the best-known figure in the world of fiction, but better known than most famous live people. It was Holmes who set the stage for the subsequent list of memorable detectives: Agatha Christie's Hercule Poirot and Jane Marple, Fred Dannay and Manfred Lee's Ellery Queen, Willard Huntington Wright's Philo Vance, Rex Stout's Nero Wolfe, Erle Stanley Gardner's Perry Mason, and a host of lesser-knowns.

But the key change in the detective story, the vital ingredient that produced the mystery story we know today, the game of Find the Villain, came after Doyle. In the Doyle tales, as in Poe's, the reader stands on the sidelines watching the great man display his skills. It's like watching a magician. One can only "ooh" and "ah" at the wizardry and applaud when the trick is explained.

It was the classical period, which followed Doyle, reaching its golden age in the twenties and thirties, that changed the mystery story into the "game" we play today. It was then that the reader, instead of watching the "Great Detective" at work, was brought onstage and invited to match wits with the master. "Can you beat the detective to the solution?" became the purpose of the story, most notably expressed in the early Ellery Queen novels where, at a certain juncture in the book, the reader would be told that he, like Ellery, now had enough information in hand to solve the puzzle on his own.

In this period, the puzzle was *all* and a great game of wits was played between author and reader. Because the Fair Play rule required that the reader be given all the clues, authors tried to trick and mislead readers by misinterpreting, obscuring, even trumpeting clues, and by strewing red herrings along the way. Therefore, the resulting tales, intricate puzzles that they were, bore little relationship to real life. In addition, the genius detective had to be matched by an equally ingenious villain to make it a contest, none of which is the way of the world.

The inevitable reaction was the American, hard-boiled novel, bent on "taking murder out of the Bishop's rose garden and putting it in the gutter where it belonged," dealing with realistic crimes in realistic settings. This school of crime writing is most notably represented by the works of Dashiell Hammett and Raymond Chandler. With them, crime was presented as ugly, detectives as fallible human beings.

Other changes have taken place. The spy novel and the police procedural came into being. Various forms, from cute-young-couples to English tea-cozies, have their day. Throughout, no matter how the mystery story

3

is presented, the game Find the Villain is still played and the rules of the mystery are still obeyed.

Why does the mystery story intrigue us as it does? The elements laid out by Edgar Allan Poe were: *Crime, detection, solution.*

These elements, crime, detection, solution, seem simple enough ingredients for a storyteller. Successful stories are created of many other ingredients as well. What is it, then, about these particular ingredients that award the mystery story such a special niche in our reading habits that publishers identify certain of their offerings as "mysteries," to let potential buyers know those books belong in a special category? That libraries will have a special section of shelves, prominently positioned, labeled "Mysteries"?

This relates to the hidden agenda in all of us that leads us to those particular books and that particular type of story.

What's on that agenda?

1. We love puzzles. Give us an intellectual challenge and we rise to the bait. Crossword puzzles and bridge problems are staples of most newspapers, and countless other puzzle games are in evidence.
2. The mystery has the same appeal as the fairy tale. Both are stories of calamities, danger, and disaster, but, at the end, everything turns out all right. As the little girl, listening to the horrors of a fairy tale in the cradle of her mother's arms, relishes the tingles of fear because she knows the dragon will be slain and the prince and princess will live happily ever after, so the mystery reader settles down to enjoy, vicariously, the catastrophes that befall his hero's efforts, relaxing in the certain knowledge that the quest will succeed.
3. The mystery story is a morality play and it has the same effect upon us. It is a tale of Good versus Evil and, though Evil may enjoy many successes throughout the run of the tale, justice will ultimately triumph. Good wins and Evil is defeated.

What greater appeals to the human psyche could one want than are offered by the mystery? Shannon OCork, in her excellent "how to" book that follows, not only instructs the would-be mystery writer in the ways to success — and she speaks from personal experience, for she's been there — but she wisely stresses the one all-important point that is etched upon the Holy Grail of all aspiring writers: "NEVER SAY DIE." Never mind teachings, critiques, praise, rejection, hope, or despair. If you would become a writer, you must *write, write, write* and never stop. The prime requisite for the successful writer isn't talent, it isn't desire, it's *guts*. As long as you keep going, no matter how rocky the road, no matter how many rejections you get, no matter how often you may lose heart, there still remains ahead of you the chance for success.

The moment you stop writing, that chance is gone.

# 1. THE MURDEROUS SPIRIT

**O**f all the skills with which a person may be gifted, the ability to make up a story and write it down must be the most common, for it is only one creative step beyond the ancient and universal act of oral storytelling. And almost all of us tell stories every day:

Across your yard a neighbor calls to you. "Hey," he says, "whatever happened to poor Tom?" And without even thinking how you're going to do it, you lay down your gardening claw and strip off your gloves and walk over to the fence, and you tell him.

"My god," your neighbor says when you've finished. "Sorry to hear it, that's too bad." Or, if Tom came to bliss, your neighbor might whistle his appreciation and say with an admiring laugh, "Wouldn't you know; always coming up roses is Tom!" And then you say, heading back to your spade-work, "And how I wish my bushes would!"

And there, without a worry or a doubt or being stuck for a word, you've told a story. And if your neighbor tells Joe who tells Terry who tells, you've told a successful story. For pretty soon everyone knows about it.

*Oh no you don't*, you're saying to me now, frowning between your eyes. "That's not all there is to it, not by a long shot! If it were *that* easy, I wouldn't want to read this book. My mystery would be on the shelves or in a hundred eager hands or already made into a movie, for god's sake!"

So, yes, of course, there's *more* to it. But that's where writing a mystery starts: Someone wants to know whatever happened to poor Tom. . . .

## Romantic and Murderous Writers

Let's back up just a little.

Without being too profound and professorial about it, there are, it seems to me, two basic kinds of fiction writers, two basic expressions of writerly temperament. There is the romantic one, which pulses to the drum of love, and the murderous one, which thrills to crime and its detection. Both deal with passion, and yes, there can be love in a mystery and crime in a romance. Often there is, and this combination gives depth to a work. But, really, it is the kind of story you write that determines which aspect is emphasized. In general, for stories of romance, emotion is the main thing, while for tales of crime, reason is dominant. *Dominant*, not *only*.

Within these broad categories of romance and mystery, many variations are possible. That's one of the glories of our world's literature and one of the joys of all the written entertainments available. From a formal sonnet to a one-line gag in a stand-up nightclub act, to a three-generational saga, to a spy thriller, to *Rebecca*, someone thinks it up and writes it down. And that, in a little sentence, is what, in essence, writing is:

●◆ You think it up and you write it down.

Ah, you say. There's the difference between me writing *The Thomas Crowne Affair* and telling my neighbor what happened to poor Tom. I *know* what happened to Tom; he's my cat or my brother or my boss or my husband. What happened to poor Tom just happened. I was there. I saw it!

Yes. That is a difference between truth and fiction, between reportage and novel writing, between keeping a diary and spinning a fantasy— although this difference is more and less than it appears, as we shall see.

But for now, yes. In fiction, first you think it up. You think before you write. Truman Capote once cattily said of another good writer, "That's not writing, that's typing!" And writers everywhere instantly knew what he meant. Whether or not the snipe was true about the author so slapped, the epithet is now a classic caution. One no serious writer wants to forget.

So now, before you decide what kind of story you're going to write, decide what kind of fiction writer you are at heart: Romantic or murderous. Whichever kind, you can write a mystery if you decide to. But one of the requirements of writing a mystery that you mean to sell is that you like what it is you're doing. If the thought of an unknown shadow sluffing toward you in the dark doesn't, somehow, pique your interest, or the flash-sight of a man in a passing train window choking a fragile beauty doesn't heat your blood a little—make you want to *find that person* or *know why* he's strangling her and what *she* did to him—then maybe mystery writing is not your best bet.

●◆ Find what *thrills* you. That's a writer's first task.

The first hard question to ask yourself is: Will I enjoy this (whatever "this" turns out to be), even when it hurts?

Writing does hurt sometimes, and you should know that right up front. You've heard of writer's block, you've seen plays where writers tear up their work, and you've read of writer breakdowns. Not in the book, but in the movie version of Stephen King's scary novel, *The Shining*, there's a moment when the writer's wife takes a look at the manuscript her husband has been obsessively working on since they became winter caretakers of the shut-down summer resort hotel. He's been telling her the writing has been going wonderfully well; he's warned her to respect his privacy and not to look. But like Bluebeard's wife, finally unable to resist, she peeks. And she sees, to her horror, line upon line of one neatly typed sentence, *the same, silly sentence*, "All work and no play makes Jack a dull boy." There it is, repeated neatly, *desperately*, page after page. The husband, of course, discovers the wife with the pages in her hand and boy, is he mad!

So, yes, writing can hurt.

But if you can *use* the hurt to make the story better, then you can endure. And in time, you become a writer.

## Persistence Is the Mystery Writer's Key

When I was first starting out, I read somewhere that the way to become a writer was to sit down in a chair somewhere and start writing. In twenty years, the authority advised, I could stand up, I would be a writer. Ah, I think now, remembering this man fondly, the classic hardnose! I'll bet he was a newspaper man. Still, I liked his advice. It helped when I knew what I'd written wasn't masterful. *I'll get better*, I thought, *in time*. And I did. I'm still getting better, but along the way, some of what I wrote was *good enough to sell*, and it didn't take twenty years. So let it be with you. There's a difference, you see, between Being a Writer and writing a novel that sells. Maybe that other guy is right and in a generation from now you'll be literary-lionized, but in the meanwhile you'll have been writing and selling quite nicely, thank you. Sometimes it's all a matter of perspective. In this book, our perspective is small. We're not after Mt. Everest. We're going to write one mystery novel and then take a look at the view from there.

Criticism? Sure, you're going to get it. Rejection? Believe me, it's coming your way. These thorns and stones are part of the path. Expect them and don't die. Rant a little if you want. That helps for some. But don't take it all so seriously-and-forevermore. Learn from the criticism and rejection if you're able to, but if you're not, let it be and *go on*. Judith Rossner, author of the fine novel *Looking For Mr. Goodbar*, once told an interviewer she had never been rejected, but I don't believe her. There must have been one failed deal, one editor who "passed" on a project, someone on high who said, "Maybe next time, sweetheart." Because none of us pleases everyone all the time. So just accept that. To start, your first mystery only has to please one person other than yourself: The editor who will buy.

## Laying the Groundwork for Your First Novel

Okay, back to basics. The average mystery novel is 60,000-65,000 words; say, 240-250 pages in manuscript, figuring twenty-five lines to a page, ten words to a line.

Years from now, when you are a seasoned veteran, the task of completing a manuscript of this length may not seem too difficult. But now, before you make your first run, take some time to think. What do I like? What *thrills* me? Who were or are my heroes? What kinds of stories and novels do I read now? What did I read, raptly, as a child?

 ➻ *Why* do I want to write a mystery at all?

I'm not asking if you want to write. You must, or you would not be with me now, embarking on this adventure. Surely you want to write, and write you will. But before you begin, peer into your soul. There, secrets lie. There, stories abound. Therein is the story of what happened to poor Tom.

For instance, what do you read first in the newspaper? Sensational crime or the style page? Political crises or the sports section? Any answer is all right; we're not talking school grades here. I'm asking you to take stock of who you are, because who you are will determine not only what you write, but how you write and what you'll write about.

Right now, while you read, why not take a notebook, a fresh, brand-new writer's notebook and start jotting down "favorite" things. Books you loved as a child and perhaps still do. Your best-loved fairy tales and nursery rhymes. Memories of best times. Childhood dreams. Look to your fantasies — they are fuel for your stories and they will reveal much that is intimate and hidden. *Things you never realized till now* — that's one way stories start. Consider what makes your heart drum with excitement, when and why your pulse flutters dangerously in your veins. What just-a-little kinky sexual experience do you fantasize alone in your bed? What comforts do you seek? Of what are you afraid?

Are you athletic and physical, or intellectual and aesthetic? At a social gathering, do you notice bodies first, or reputations? Do you want to meet the archaeologist, the NBC White House reporter, Bill's new wife, or the local marathon runner? Do you tinker with electronics gear, restore old houses, or spend expensive hours at a beauty shop being professionally done? What do you watch on television? How about your musical taste: Do you like to downtown boogie till the milkman walks, or do you listen to symphonies on compact disc? Do you have a dog, a sophisticated tank with fish, or do you live in a pet-less home with a plate collection precisely aligned upon a wall?

Look at your life. How is it structured? Of what does it consist? Where do you run when you're frightened? What do you run to when you want love? What do you *lack* — and yearn for?

Becoming a writer is not only repetitious workdays spent setting down a tale, fulfilling your daily quota of words. (Though it is that. Oh yes, becoming a writer is work all right, and we'll come to that.) But it is also a contemplation of the self, a meditative way of life, for in setting down *whatever*, a writer is revealed to herself as well as to others, and to others the most clearly. And so — and this *is* profound — a writer writes what she can. Only what she can.

●◆ A writer writes only what he or she can.

To write a mystery then, a writer needs to know something of what he is. And he needs, in some measure, "the murderous spirit."

This does not mean that mystery writers are mean-spirited, outlaw types secretly hating the world and all of us in it.

To the contrary. The mystery writer is, by nature, the sweetest writer of them all. The mystery writer is in touch with his killer instinct. The mystery writer acknowledges the darkness in himself without shame, so the blood runs out of it. Cleansed, it can be used. Artistically used. Creatively used. *Exploited*. Pure of heart, *but in touch with the sinister*, we write . . . and write well. Evil is punished at last. The innocent are freed from their oppression and life's terrible obstacles are cleared away. Goodness triumphs when all is blackest, just as the villain's knife flies toward the beauty's throat.

Ah, how good.

We had an exciting ride, all whips and screeches and doom and thrills. The simple life we come back to looks better for the taste of the bad and the wild we had *out there, as in a dream*. Animals all, we remember the wicked. It is a part of us, deep in the oldness of our bones. It is a part we need to exercise, from time to time, to keep it slumbering.

So seek your murderous spirit. Don't be ashamed. Get it out of whatever secret closet you stuffed it into and put it shining on your desk. Groom it, nourish it. It's the first tool you're going to use writing your mystery, and it's the most important one you need.

# 2. MYSTERY SUBGENRES AND SITUATIONS

The mystery novel, the kind you're writing, the kind that sets forth a crime and its detection as the story, is not really very old. It began as a short story a little over a hundred years ago, and it is just now really hitting its stride. Novels of "romantic suspense" are older, but more popular than ever. New York editors say we are coming into a "second golden age" for all types of mystery novels. It is the most popular form of entertainment literature today, worldwide.

And as a genre, it's a rainbow. Here, quickly, are some of the mystery's colors.

## The Amateur Detective

Sherlock Holmes, you know. Everyone knows Sherlock Holmes. He is first in the pantheon of crime-detectors and always will be. But there are many others and there is room for yours.

The amateur detective is usually, though not always, male. Probably because, until lately, men had the reputation of being brighter than women. These masterminds usually follow the model as first laid down by Poe. They are, as a rule, of independent income or at least able to sample life's opportunities at their whim, due to a particular happy circumstance. And they are, almost by definition, eccentric in some intellectually superior way: C. Auguste Dupin, Poe's odd Parisian gentleman, for instance, disliked the light of day to the extent of keeping all the windows shuttered in his "time-eaten and grotesque" mansion, lighting his interiors with "strongly perfumed" candles. Only at night did he willingly venture out to seek, Poe writes, "that infinity of mental excitement which quiet observation can afford." You may find a more modern parallel in the aversion of Rex Stout's Nero Wolfe to stepping beyond the front door of his Manhattan brownstone, and in his passion for cultivating orchids.

Usually, too, the amateur detective has an encyclopedic mind and wide-ranging interests. Sherlock Holmes knew the different treads of bicycle tires, for heaven's sake, as well as the genetic conditions necessary for red hair, without having to look them up. So, something peculiar and much extraordinary marks the genius amateur.

And these masterminds usually have a "Boswell," a partner or confidant who is the narrator and who, while humbling himself, extols the superiority of the mastermind, as the amateur detective pits his wits against the fiendish, almost-as-good mind of the villain of the story. The villain is usually "identity unknown" until the climax, and the villain's identity, by reader expectation, should be a surprise. In the late twenties there was the tremendously popular Philo Vance of Willard Huntington Wright, who wrote his mystery series as though each were reports of true crime. The narrator is Philo Vance's secretary, his Watson. He is called "Van," and the novels are authored, pseudonymously, by S. S. Van Dine. Later, in England, Agatha Christie's Hercule Poirot had Dr. Hastings to tell his story.

It is interesting to note that when Dame Agatha gave us Miss Jane Marple, she wrote, most of the time, in the objective third person. Jane Marple, if not the first female mastermind, was the best of her time, and she is almost the opposite of the male genius-sleuth. Miss Marple is unpretentious. Therefore, she is underestimated by almost everyone concerned with the crime. She dithers about and says seemingly silly feminine things. Men rush to help her up from deep armchairs and to retrieve her knitting. She doesn't use bad language or have fistfights, but Jane Marple, too, is one of the immortals.

## The Cozy

The Miss Marple novels, although they are of the amateur detective school, are called cozies. And so are the many others of like kind. In the cozy, the violence is muted, the characters are usually urbane and civilized. They dress for dinner, they have servants (or would if they could afford to), and they rarely shout. Often the murders take place on country week-ends at fine estates or in some such other cosseted atmosphere. In *The Murder at the Vicarage*, Miss Marple's debut novel, a rich man is murdered in the study of a village vicar. Cozies are often called "indoor" mysteries because even though one victim or many may be murdered outside, the whole read is gentle, witty, and "dressed." They are popular in their English flavor and in their New England one, but they are ready and waiting to be thoroughly Americanized.

## The Puzzle

Puzzle mysteries usually feature a series hero or heroine, and, in essence, the whole novel is laid out to display the ingenuity of the "gimmick" used for the murder, which, in the best of them, also points indisputably to the villain's guilt. John Dickson Carr was famous for his "locked-door" puzzle mysteries. In his novel, *The Hollow Man*, he has his hero, Dr. Gideon Fell, develop a fulsome lecture on the subject. In this now famous lecture, Dr. Fell reveals his choice for a prime example of this kind of mystery, Melville Davisson Post's *The Doomdorf Mystery*. Obscure now, and maybe even in 1935 when Dr. Fell first mentioned it, *The Doomdorf Mystery* nevertheless serves as a definitive example of its kind:

> . . . and the long-range assassin is the sun. The sun strikes through the window of the locked room, makes a burning-glass of a bottle of Doomdorf's own raw white wood-alcohol liquor on the table, and ignites through it the percussion cap of a gun hanging on the wall: so that the breast of the hated one is blown open as he lies in his bed.

Erle Stanley Gardner's Perry Mason made a consummate success of the puzzle, which is not so fashionable today—their ilk seems to have gone to television episodes. This kind of mystery needs updating to regain its audience, a new champion created by a fresh writer with a new bag of magician's tricks in contemporary settings.

## The Private Detective

This subgenre is distinctly American, the detective is the hard-boiled tough egg. Dashiell Hammett got him right with Sam Spade, though before him there was Earl Derr Biggers' Charlie Chan. Raymond Chandler's Philip Marlow perfected the model, and writers ever since the forties have been having a field day with America's own contribution to mysteries, the private eye. He's an Everyman hero, an alienated loner of high principle, tough muscle, and wisecracking tone. Unmarried, he knows that sexually appealing women are never to be trusted and are always trouble. Sometimes, though, he has a sisterly type female who works for him, looks after him, and loves him hopelessly from afar, such as Sam Spade's Effie Perine. This "good girl" might even be brainy. American mystery novels will never be through with this guy. He's too much "us" and he's so good, though he's changing too. John D. MacDonald's Travis McGee ate up women like rare steaks; Robert B. Parker's Spenser is faithful to his girlfriend. Mickey Spillane's Mike Hammer didn't even have to reach out for his women. They came running so often, slipping out of their clothes, he had to literally fight them off. Today, Dick Francis' detectives, both amateur and professional, sometimes have trouble getting kissed.

Editors say they are tired of the private eye, but he's still very popular with readers. And these days "he" can be female. In fact, these days he often is.

## The Police Procedural

From the private eye, it wasn't too big a jump to the professional police detective. In the forties, the police procedural was born. Lawrence Treat first did it, then Hillary Waugh, Ed McBain, and Joseph Wambaugh. In these mysteries, the procedures of deduction utilize the professional methods and scientific techniques of the police investigator. The hero is underplayed. He is a company man, preferring to use authorized means to catch the villain, rather than, as Mickey Spillane's Mike Hammer did, acting with private rage and sometimes illegal methods.

In Hillary Waugh's classic *Last Seen Wearing*, for example, Police Chief Frank Ford of a little New England town searches for a missing young woman. Half the book is spent in a painstaking search, elaborately detailed. When he finally finds the woman, she is dead, and Chief Ford and his men must plod on, slowly accruing information. The credit for the ultimate solution and capture of the murderer belongs as much to investigative analysis as to Chief Ford's keen deductions. The police procedural is very modern, reducing the role of the mastermind detective to that of able professional, but, as we would wish in real life, a professional of the highest moral probity.

## The Romantic Suspense

This kind of mystery deals, often, with mainstream themes of love, life, happiness, and "good people" just trying to get through this life but falling, through no fault of their own, into terrible jeopardy. Usually the main character is a woman who is sexually appealing and unprotected. If these novels are set in the past, they could be called gothics, but a true gothic needs a grand old mansion, a wild moor, and a dark and stormy night. Daphne du Maurier's *Rebecca*, in which a second wife finds herself haunted by what she thinks is her husband's love of his dead first wife and then discovers that instead the husband hated the first enough to murder her, may be the best of these. There is something sexual in the mystery of suspense that stirs and frightens readers—mostly women—in the most delicious way.

## The Thriller

Usually the thriller novel is a "spy-thriller." There's much danger and action back and forth between continents. Often it is the free world the hero is trying to save, and usually the violence is sophisticated and sly. Good country is pitted against bad, using gadgets, state-of-the-art technological machines. The latest scientific theory and engineering advances are built into the chase scenes and the mayhem. There are often speeding cars, boats, airplanes, or helicopters, and there are clever killing tools such as Ian Fleming's James Bond used—a briefcase that fires bullets with laser-like precision or some such wondrous device. In the thriller, the world is the hero's fighting field and the climaxes are often world wars or the stopping of one. This kind of mystery is, like the novels of romantic suspense, usually better written and wider selling than the pulp-style private eye novel, but that is only a general assessment. Mystery novels of all kinds are, every day, expertly done.

The thriller uses World Wars I and II as background, perhaps as often as it uses the possibility of WW III and global annihilation, and it uses Europe, Asia, and the Middle East more than it uses America. David Cornwell, writing as John Le Carré, is today's master of the thriller, and Ken Follett is right up there with him. There are subgenres to this category. There are the techno-thrillers of Tom Clancy, which are virtual tracts on U.S. defense systems. There are thrillers of high finance and the corporate

16

world, and thrillers involving invasions by other worlds. Invent your own canvas, dream up your own villains. Today, the world is just waiting to be conquered by *something new and strange*, isn't it?

Well, there are others. There are comic caper novels and novels of psychological menace, novels of serial killers, and novels that fictionalize historical crimes. There are science fiction mysteries and adventure-action mysteries and cute couple mysteries, such as Frances and Richard Lockridge's Pam and Jerry North, and Dashiell Hammett's Nick and Nora Charles.

Choose your own. Today, the market is open. It's eager for new variations on the old, and it's looking for what's brand-new. Do your own kind of mystery; start a subgenre of your own. Or master the well-marked paths laid down by those who went before. Either way, you can write a fine, saleable mystery.

Whatever you know, whatever you like, however you write best, if you want to, you can make a mystery out of it. You can have a hero or heroine you like so well you'll want to write him into another story and so start a series. Or you can start fresh each time. You can put your mystery in the modern day or in the past or the future. You can be on land, in water or the air, or even on another planet in a ghostly galaxy.

There's no "you-can't" in the mystery. The cobwebbed door creaks open for us all. Beyond, something shimmers and beckons with pale finger.

Come on. Let's go in after it.

## Developing a Mystery Situation

We all have some bad feelings and wretched memories we don't want, or are not ready, to deal with today. That's fine. We're going to write a mystery novel, not go into psychoanalysis. Fondling your murderous spirit should be fun, not hurtful. Not yet. Years from now you may turn back to a truly climactic time of your life and explore it to weave a wonderful work. But you probably won't. Really traumatic experiences usually reveal themselves in different ways and in analogous situations you use without knowing it.

I know a man whose first child died in its fifth year. It is not something he chooses to think of often because now, years later, the pain is still alive. He compensates by being overly kind, lax even, to his other children. How it happened he has not told me. But I can use his experience, as little as I know of it, to write a mystery. Just this one little fact, unexplained, and around it I—or you—could write a book. It wouldn't be Tom's story. Of course not. We don't *want* Tom's story, we want our own. Ours will be better.

Let's see now. There is a man, a neighbor of the narrator. He is still suffering years later from the sudden, unexpected death of his first child. Why? The marriage did not survive long after either. He blamed his bride for the child's demise; she blamed him. At any rate, within two years he married again, a more wealthy woman, a young socialite. Ummm. . . . And the first offspring of that second union is named for the first child, the new mother not knowing the tragic association? Of course, some time later she finds out. And then *the second child* is seriously injured. Though the child survives, she is not the same. She loses her bright intelligence, her looks, her gentle disposition. She grows to adulthood plain and surly and accident-prone. When the child is twenty-one, the parents separate. The husband blames the collapse of this marriage on the child coming constantly between him and his wife. . . . Ah, we're thinking out a mystery!

This is a situation only, not yet a plot. But how many different mystery novels could this simple situation spawn?

Give it a thought. How would you write *Whatever Happened to Poor Tom*? Tom, after all, could be a woman's name, a nickname of some kind. In this age of androgyny, don't let a name limit you. Use it for your own devious designs. . . .

Who would be the villain? The man, the first bride, the second wife, the second child? You could do it any of those ways. You could, but it would be harder, make the first baby the villain. You know—the child didn't really die, but was stolen and hidden away somewhere. She grew into a monster, insinuating herself, unknown to the man, into his life as (1) an anonymous hate-letter writer, (2) a spying neighbor, (3) the narrator of the story, told by the "best friend" of the second child. The first begotten really hates the half-sibling and causes "the injury."

You think up one. It isn't so hard and it's fun. The point I'm making is that this "murderous spirit" you're polishing and getting to know and love doesn't have to be inner-directed. Send it out to look at the world, your immediate world. Forget for the moment the big global canvas. Starting out, let's think small and precisely. We can always balloon our idea, make things bigger once we've worked it out—and our ballooning ideas will hold and fly beautifully if our structure is good. But if it isn't, all could crash. So for now, let's build only a skeleton, a simple little skeleton, only bones and balance.

## A Word About Ethics

And now what have I done, building a story around someone I know? I've got you thinking about your neighbors! So let's talk about ethics.

Does a writer have the right to examine the outward facts of other people's personalities and lives and use them for the writer's purposes? Yes. But a qualified yes. Like many other good things, it's more *how* you do it than that you do. All writers do it. Of course. We have to. But you cannot invade their privacy or make attacks on an actual person's character. Libel laws protect private citizens from such abuse. This side of writing from real-life is discussed more completely on pages 60-61.

Whether you write a fantasy tale or a realistic novel, life as you know it is where you start. You have to, to be able to communicate with your reader. Life and all its stories, untold and overtold, are what connect us to each other. Friend to friend, stranger to stranger, ancestor to great-grand-child—what's *out there* is our first common meeting ground (what's *in here* is the second), and every person in this world who knew about poor Tom would want to know what happened to him. It's innate, our human curiosity. It's instinctual, our need to know each other. Everyone loves stories. Stories entertain, they teach, they comfort, they thrill. Stories are companions and secret best friends. Stories are a form of socializing. They are love letters and exhortations and cautionary tales. *Stories* are why we read and what we read for. The desire to remember a good story exactly is one of the reasons alphabets, inks, and pens were invented. And the urge to tell a good story to someone—anyone—is why you are going to write a mystery novel.

> ➥ As sure as there are rocks in New England, we are writing not only for ourselves, *but to give pleasure, in some way, to other people.*

19

# The Doing Is the Thing

And now a word on a private pleasure, the beholding of your first mystery as a published, actual object. Oh yes, it is very fine to write a mystery, send it off and have it bought, and then see it appear in print with your name attached to it. But here's a truth: It is not as fine as you imagine.

I remember anticipating the thrill of triumphantly holding my first book in my hands. I thought that nothing could be grander. But when that special day came and I held my first novel, completed, shiny, *priced*, I felt very little. Instead of seeing it as something I created, I saw it as something I might or might not buy; I saw it as if I were a prospective reader, and seeing it so made it seem an all right thing, but not a celebration. As soon as it was itself and on its own, I saw it as something different and no longer mine but only of me, and what I wanted then was not to hold it but for someone, *everyone*, to buy it.

In truth, the celebration had come before. It was a long, interminable-seeming time from word of acceptance to contract and check, and then to galleys and then to dust jacket and then to actual book. I had been a year and a half writing it, two years selling it; it had been a year in the publishing house in preparation. By that time I was ending another novel, one that interested me much more than the completed one. One that I was sure was much better and which would make me famous.

That first work had, without my realizing it, become yesterday. But that's the writing game too. Come on along.

The fun, the wonder, the grandeur, the sublimity of it all comes to an author at different places and different times, and is much too short-lived. James M. Cain, who wrote, among others, the classics *The Postman Always Rings Twice* and *Double Indemnity*, said his favorite work changed with the royalty checks; he liked best whichever one earned him the most. Late in his life his favorite work was *Rainbow's End*, little known today. It was his last. The publishers paid for his reputation up front; the book he wrote was not his best. But it paid for his old age and so it topped his list.

•◆ The journey, the doing is the thing.

So let it be with you.
And now let's get down to it.

# 3. PLOT: THE VITAL IDEA

The vital idea, the plot, is the *brain* of your mystery. It's not the skeleton; the skeleton is the structure you build from your plot. The plot is the story you're telling. It's not all—it's never all—and by itself it has no life. Your writing fleshes it out; your characters, your incidents, your pace give it blood and pulse. But the plot is the *without which, nothing*. So before you start piling up your daily pages, you want to have your plot.

➤ A plot is a situation carried through to a fitting conclusion.

Yes, some writers maintain they don't need a plot to start. What they start with, as we studied in chapter 2, is *situation*:

*Let's see*, one thinks: A little girl drowns in a pond. She went after her cat on what she thought was hard ice and she fell through. Her friend tried to save her and fell in too, but survived because a woman in the house that overlooked the pond happened to look out her window and see two bright wool caps, one red, one blue, bobbing on the surface of the water where the ice was broken down.

I can write that scene, the writer says, and he sits down and he writes it. Chapter one. And as he sails along, ideas run in his mind; *possibilities*. He mumbles and he mutters, happily thinking *what if*. The pages mount. His characters begin forming, as out of fog. He writes on, working from the vague to the concrete, tacking in, tacking out, beyond sight of shore. Chapters roll by. Everyone becomes a suspect while he tries out different solutions. In time he's got it the way he wants it; land has been sighted. He's at the climax of his tale, in a tailwind, and the harbor looms. He slips into port with a flourish, he does a spiffy job. Then he cleans up. He goes back over his completed first draft, straightens out the wrong turns, truesup the inconsistencies of his characters to fit his ending, and he's ready for printout and the market.

But this writer is a working pro. You, the first time out, don't want to write a mystery this way, because without a worked-up plot, with only a situation to send you out, you start weak. Don't do that. Give yourself every chance for success; start from strength. Think out your possibilities before you start. That writer up above was seasoned and confident. He knew how to go over the bounding main; he'd been out there before. This first time, start with a thought-out, well-reasoned plot. Make your mistakes in outline. They're easy to spot in outline. They're easier to correct.

●➤ Your outline is your map. You're going to have a plot, and you're going to outline it before you take off.

When I was struggling through my first plot outline, I made just about every mistake a writer could. First, I suffered from perfectionism. No plot was good enough for me. My plot had to be clever and fresh, dazzling in resolution and presentation. It had to be original, a trick never done before. It had to have every character a suspect, and I had so many suspects. It had to. . . . And there I was, bleeding and not writing. Only an instant classic would do, and since I wasn't up to writing a classic then, eh?, I *wasn't writing*.

If I'd kept that up I'd have been a fatality like the others in my writing class. Worse than them, I'd never have begun, much less finished. Be smarter than me. You're going to think up a plot, an appropriate plot, and that's going to be that. You're going to give it a background you know and therefore can handle. You're going to sparsely populate it with the kind of people you're familiar with. You're going to keep the time frame short so your mystery has immediacy—immediacy is easier than sweep. You don't want to write, first time, a sinister 300,000-word saga. You're going to write your first draft with care all the way to the finish, and then you'll rewrite with flair.

Here is your plot: *Something happens, how and why.*

Something happens: *That's a situation.*

How and why: *That's a plot.*

The rest is writing, fiction writing. The rest is subplots and red herrings (false trails), threat and suspense and local color and character development, the whole whipped together into a tempting sauce so tasty the reader eats it all thinking he's only after the meat.

Because you're writing a mystery, the something that happens will involve murder or the threat of murder or the appearance of murder. A mystery without a murder lacks blood. Oh yes, you can have a mystery about other crimes. Kidnapping. Rape. Embezzlement. Grand theft. And many wonderful mysteries have been written about these crimes. But all serious crimes tend toward murder, they point toward it in a way. Murder is society's worst crime, the most feared, the most punished, the most abhorred by civilized peoples. Murder is what, *if you're really bad*, you do. And murder is the most common, the *easiest* of crimes. Murder is the one crime we all share. Anybody can do it . . . and might. *We've all wanted to.*

"I hate you," a child, denied something, screams at her father. "I'm going to *kill* you." What if she did?

"I wish you'd *die*," the employee, reprimanded by a disliked superior, thinks silently to himself, slinking back to his desk. What if his superior did?

"I'd win this beauty contest," grumbles a competitor to her mother, "if only Felicity wasn't in it." What if Felicity wasn't?

"Frank would marry me in a minute," dreams Barbara, "if I wasn't already married to John." What if Barbara were suddenly a widow?

"If that woman nags me one more time about staying too long in my workroom, I'm going to bash her head in," broods a henpecked husband. What if his wife nags him that one more time?

You could plot a fine mystery out of any of these simple situations.

Every day come moments of crisis, and our predator minds turn, by nature, to killing. Oh, we don't mean it, you say. Don't we? For one wonderful wild moment, *don't we?* . . . Sure we do. We just don't act on it, most of us. We deny it, bury it, repudiate it. We reflect, and reason returns. Our blood quiets down, we consider the consequences. The anger fades. We change our minds about father, mother, rival, husband, wife; we like them again. Most of the time.

But every day, murders happen.

And most murders are committed upon people known to the murderer. It's really frightening, when you think about it, just how vulnerable we all are. You argue with your husband and go to bed in the guest room. You're not used to the sharp corners of that room and the new bed is strange. You

shift in the darkness, lie there hating your mate, what a monster he is. . . .
And then finally you fall into a light sleep and hear, on the edge of waking,
someone tiptoeing into the room. It's John, you think, though menace
quivers in the air. It must be John, mustn't it . . . who else could it be? . . .
*And what is he after now? . . .*

Plots, reduced to their essence, don't usually look so grand. The trick
is in the telling, the particularizing, the fleshing out.

Here's a plot: There is something of value, and more than one person
wants it. They all try to obtain it in devious ways. Some die in the pursuit,
and they all lose out in the end. The something of value gets away. The
hero is the only one among them who doesn't want it.

Not too exciting? Not too exquisitely clever? Well, that's the plot of
Dashiell Hammett's *The Maltese Falcon*, maybe the most famous mystery
novel of them all.

Here's another. Here, just for instance, let's say, is your plot, built on
the situation at the beginning of this chapter:

Because *B* has found out *A*'s terrible secret, *A* murders *B* and makes it
look like an accident. *C* doesn't know the accident is really a murder, but
cared about *B* and wants to know how the accident happened. So *C* snoops
around and frightens *A* into thinking *C* must be murdered too. *C* doesn't
suspect *A*; there's no reason to. *C* suspects *D*. Following *D*, not knowing
the truth, *C* comes to the climax where *A* can kill *C*. *D* is in trouble in the
climax too. *C* must either let *D* die or save *D*. *C*, believing *D* is the killer,
almost lets *D* go, but finally saves *D* and in so doing saves himself because
saving the other somehow foils *A*'s diabolical plan. At the end, *D* is proven
innocent, *C* learns how *B* was killed, and *A* comes to justice, the truth all
out. *A* either dies trying to kill *C* or is apprehended, and life for the others
goes on, perhaps to a sequel if you think *C* might be a good series hero.

A hundred mysteries and more, some good, some less so, could be
written to this formula or variations thereof. In particular, they would all
be different. In how they were done, they would either be successful or
not.

**⇥** *Plots. Every mystery has two.* At least two.

First, there's the real story. That's the one you're hiding under the second, the *apparent* story. The apparent story is the one that shows. But as
you unwind the apparent one, the real one *begins to show through*. That's

24

exciting. There's intense reader curiosity and excitement and even a little delicious *dread*, much like unwrapping a mummy in a musty, golden tomb. Oh, the thrill of it! A little at a time, one chapter at a time, the *hidden is unraveled* until . . . at last . . . the mummy's eyes are set free of the winding cloth . . . and what is exposed is *recognized*!

That's the trick you're up to. You, the writer. And that's the fun of a mystery novel for the reader. The reader gets two-for-one. The reader knows there's a prize in the box of Cracker Jacks you've given him. While he hunts for it, he smacks his lips through the goodies you've filled the box with. The goodies keep him going. He searches happily on. Before he knows it he's gotten to the bottom, and he fingers the surprise in the darkness there. Eager, he draws it up. . . .

And if he liked what he got, he'll go right out and buy your next mystery, and you've got your writing career going.

## Developing a Sample Plot and Characters

Let's say that you, the author of a mystery-to-be, work, in real life, part-time in a grocery store. And now, sitting down to work up your mystery's vital idea, so far what you have is only your formula, all dull *ABCs*. You've got your idea, not even a fully explored situation yet: A little girl drowns in a pond, only it's not an accident, it's murder. You haven't got your *motive* yet (the reason why), but you have your *means*, death by drowning in an iced-over pond. Well, you've got the kernel of your means; you still have to figure out how a murder could be committed in this seemingly accidental way. And you're started on your *opportunity*, which is the moment when your murderer is able to make the crime take place.

- *Motive, means, and opportunity*: Every mystery has to explain these. Motive, means, and opportunity are your linchpins; they secure the wheel of your plot so you can spin it. We'll come to these, but first we have to invent our wheel.

*A* is the seemingly good neighbor, the little old lady who looked out her window and saw the children's caps bobbing in the pond.

*B* is the little girl who chased her cat and went too far out on the ice and broke through and drowned.

*C* is the mother of the other child who also fell in.

*D* is the other child. He lived through the incident. He's the stepson, let's say, of *C*.

That wasn't so hard, was it? And, you know, this idea is already beginning to look interesting. What we've done here is put *C*, the hero of the mystery, in dual jeopardy. First, according to our formula, *C* must come to suspect her own stepson of murdering the victim. Second, *C* will be in real danger from the little old lady who saved *C*'s stepson so *C* could suspect him! *Oh, I like this*, you think to yourself. And if you do, so will others. You're rolling.

Now, just for juice, let's have an *E*. *E* is the father of the murdered little girl.

That's enough situation and cast of characters for an excellent mystery.

## Motive

Here comes the hard part. We need a motive for why the old lady would kill a neighbor's child. *What could bring the woman to that point?*

Let's forget insanity, because insanity isn't reasonable. What is *reasonable* is more frightening and interesting than what isn't. Insanity can't be motivated or sympathized with or understood or seen through. You want a motive your readers will understand and accept. You want something like greed (great gain), or terror (the victim would have got me if I didn't get him first). Or both.

We start then with *A*, our murderer in the guise of Good Samaritan. Her name is Martha Smith, Miss Martha Smith. She's a spinster, the town's longtime elementary school math teacher, now retired. She taught our hero, *C*, when *C* was young, and our romantic interest, *E*. Miss Smith lives in a lovely house on the property where the pond is. She owns the property; clever all her life and very good at mathematics, she invested well in the market, she claims, and lives very comfortably in her old age. With no children of her own, she offers the use of her pond in winter for the town children to skate on. She has a groundskeeper who is supposed to watch over the pond and tend to it and put up the sign when the ice is frozen thick enough to be safe for skating.

This is the apparent story. What's the real one?

Our villain, Miss Martha Smith, is too clever by half. In the early sixties, she realized she could make a very good living dealing drugs to schoolchildren. She couldn't do it herself, of course, so she had an accomplice.

Perhaps he was her lover. He showed her the ropes, taught her a source of supply. She put up the initial investment money, he skulked around the schoolyard. They did well. In time he got caught and was sent away. He did not tell on her. In fact, he is the current groundskeeper, returned after serving his time and so changed by prison life that no one recognizes him. Of course, he changed his name and lives virtually as a recluse. At least he doesn't socialize in the town, which we'll place in a state we know. For me that would be Connecticut. I'll call the town Land's Rest.

Though the groundskeeper lives in a small cabin on the Smith property, he has always been Miss Smith's lover. And he still (or once again) is the town's drug dealer, only he's more cautious now. He uses high school boys, who do not know who he is, as his intermediaries. He deals with them only in darkness, a mask over his face.

But one day, *B*, the little girl victim, finds out who and what the groundskeeper really is and lets him know she knows. He, not as smart as Miss Smith, goes to the former math teacher and tells her he has been "unmasked." Miss Smith says she'll take care of it. She loves this man, has loved him all her life. She waited for him through her best years; he is all the world to her. And Miss Smith knows that if the groundskeeper is exposed, he'll face time in prison as a second offender. He will not be able to take incarceration a second time around. She'll lose him and he'll break. This time he will tell on her—he'll make a deal with the authorities to save himself. And she cannot face the public exposure of what she is. After all, Martha Smith is one of the shining pillars in this town.

So she decides to kill little *B* so things can go on as they have been.

All right. Now we have motive.

- ◆◆ Start your plot with the murderer's motive. Work that out right away and make it strong.
- ◆◆ From motive, we move to *means*.

As we go, you'll notice, we're fleshing out our characters almost without struggle. Things just seem to start fitting in. We let them. We don't concentrate on fine details now; that will come when we *characterize*.

## Means

Once you've established your villain's motive, it's time to work out the means—in this case, how Miss Smith will drown *B* in the pond.

To do this, we have to particularize our situation and our characters; as we go, we'll find a way.

So let's give *B* a name now, a likeable name because we want our victim, this time, to be mourned. Neddy. That's a cute nickname for a thirteen-year-old girl. Thirteen is old enough to know what's what, but young enough to be still vulnerable in life. Neddy's given name is Edwina Claire Chance. She's her father's darling. He's divorced, and for reasons generally unknown because he doesn't talk about them, he has sole custody of her. And since we've named her, let's name her father too. His name will be Donovan Chance. He's a college professor who works at a university thirty miles away. His field should be a subject you know something about; let's say modern English literature.

Wasting no time, we go back to Miss Smith who is deciding how to rid herself of little Neddy. We've got the pond as a given, and Miss Smith's lending of it during the winter to the children. We've got the man responsible for the safety of the pond wanting to sink little Neddy too. And the pond idea is fresh — it hasn't been done in any mystery you've read lately. The wintry landscape can lend some nice shivery atmosphere. So Neddy will be lured out onto thin ice in some way and fall through in some way that will seem a plausible accident.

Okay, now to the how. Let's make little Neddy want to be an Olympic skater. She sees every ice show she can; Katarina Witt and Dorothy Hamill are her role models. Her father, Donovan Chance, supports his daughter's ambition, encouraging her in it. The Chances live close to Smith Pond, on the same country road, as does the as-yet-unnamed *C* family. So Neddy often skates early in the morning before most of the other children are up and dressing for school, and she skates late on winter evenings after the other children go home. She has been forbidden to skate on the pond if no one is there to watch over her. That's why, that fatal day, her friend *D* is with her.

This, too, will serve to work out the way Neddy discovered the truth about the groundskeeper. Her father pays the groundskeeper a small stipend to keep an eye on Neddy when she skates in the evenings, and the groundskeeper can't resist tempting the aspiring young skater to try amphetamine. It will improve her performance, he says, give her zip and stamina. Neddy talks this over with her school friend, *D*, who is one of the town boys recruited by the groundskeeper as a dealer.

## Brainstorms

I've had a brainstorm. These unplanned ideas come from who-knows-where and who-knows-when. They come up out of the well of one's mind somehow, and they are usually fortuitous, so grab on to them if you can. I'll talk about brainstorms in a minute. Just let me tell you what mine was.

Clementine. Going through the unused-up initials of the alphabet looking for a name for the groundskeeper, I thought of Clementine. Remember the old folk song, "My Darling Clementine"? She lost her footing, fell into a "foaming brine," and was lost to the singer of the song forevermore. He tolls it a "dreadful sorrow." This is good. We'll change our thirteen-year-old victim's nickname from Neddy to Clemmy, and her full name from Edwina Claire to Edwina Clementine Chance. We'll work in the old folk song; that will give our contemporary plot *resonance*, an association with folklore. Our mystery has just gained a depth it didn't have before.

- Brainstorms, or happy accidents that enrich some aspect of your story, come. They just come. We can't plan for them, we can't count on them, sometimes they just happen. I don't know why and never know when. But when one comes, it gives me assurance. It seems that when I'm working right, a few drop in. The "brainstorm" makes a better piece of work, always. All writers are grateful for them, and to all of us, they're mysteries. Some are bigger than others, some are better than others, but if you get one, use it. Think of it as a good omen. You're in correct alignment with your universe. You're working right.

And we're still figuring out our *means* and, along with that, our *opportunity*.

## Further Developing Your Characters

The groundskeeper's name is Rey Hermanas. It used to be Frankie deSpain. He's Mexican and sexy. He's dark and muscular and fit. The reader will understand why Miss Martha Smith loves him so. He's not truly handsome, but he has a real charm. We'll make this villain a man who has always been liked by both men and women. Rey is not intellectually superior, but he is easy and affable. Mature now (we'll make him fifty-five), he's laid-back, self-sufficient, dependable, and polite. He keeps to himself, doesn't bother anybody. Lots of the women in Land's Rest look on him with interest and he's a wee bit mysterious because he pays none of them any mind. They don't know he has his love, you see. But the guy's a lady-killer; I'm in love with him already. And he got fit in prison. When he went away long ago he was bearded and unkempt, stocky, and twenty years younger.

*D*, whose name is Gabriel Gorham, will be a problem child. Clemmy is thirteen, Gabriel is fifteen. He is the only child of *C*'s husband, who died of a brain tumor in the second year of his marriage to *C*. That left *C* to raise a stepson who has not accepted her yet. Gabriel's mother died a suicide; she was an alcoholic beauty with a brooding disposition. Let's smooth this out.

*C*, our heroine. Her name is Aurora Lyons Gorham, and she's twenty-eight. At twenty-five, three years ago, she married Gabriel's father, Jonathan Gorham. Aurora, called Ror, was a nurse. She met Jonathan when he was a patient of hers. She knew the risks of his illness and married him anyway. Jonathan's son, Gabriel Gorham, resented Ror. His mother died when he was ten, his father had a successful brokerage business, and the boy was raised by a live-in domestic. He was spoiled. His father spent too little time with him and compensated with material gifts.

Gabriel has become the kind of privileged "good boy who goes wrong" out of parental neglect or lack of proper family life. This was one of the reasons Jonathan Gorham begged Aurora to marry him though he was seriously ill—he wanted to secure a good mother for his boy. And this is one of the reasons Aurora married Jonathan Gorham. Yes, she loved him, but she knew she would probably be a widow young. She thought that Gabriel needed her, and he does, but from the first he has spurned her attempts to be friends. Gabriel accuses Ror of marrying his father for money.

Gabriel looked down on Aurora because, as a nurse, she was socially beneath him in his eyes. He is a very hurt boy. After his father died, he and Aurora were thrown together, and she has had her hands full with him ever since. He needs Ror, but doesn't want to.

Now he has fallen in with bad companions. He thinks he has become hip and street smart by dealing drugs to the schoolchildren of Land's Rest High School. Though Ror does not know Gabriel is dealing, she knows he's rarely home and that she can't control him, and she has decided to send him to a boarding school in the spring. He knows this and has told her he will never go. They live in one of the fine houses on Winter Lane in an uneasy alliance. Gabriel's one friend is Clemmy Chance. Clemmy is all things pure and beautiful to Gabriel; he loves her with all his young heart.

And then, though he tries to save Clemmy when she falls through the ice, he loses her too.

So Gabriel is in the hospital, very ill, suffering from the aftereffects of hypothermia and almost drowning. And he is in despair. He has lost, so young, his mother and his father and his "sweetheart." All he has are his hated stepmother and his resentments. He lies in his hospital bed refusing to talk. And yes, his hated stepmother acts as his nurse; because of her nursing skills she takes one eight-hour shift of the three that tend him around the clock.

Piece by piece, see how it grows?

But we still haven't nailed down our *means* and *opportunity*. So we'll go back and see what we've got. We'll line it all up, make some sense of things thus far, and set in our murder scene.

### Fleshing Out the Plot

Right away I see we have to fit in the author's supermarket background. All right. We'll make the supermarket the place—the parking lot behind it—where Gabriel meets his supplier, groundskeeper Rey Hermanas, after dark, and where Gabriel sells drugs to his customers. We'll also make the supermarket the place where the townspeople in the novel meet and gossip, and where Clemmy accidentally discovers the truth about Rey Hermanas.

Clemmy notices that Miss Martha Smith buys a lot of cat food. She notices because Clemmy has a cat named Double Axel for whom she buys food, and she always seemed to be running into Miss Smith at the cat food display. And Miss Smith, Clemmy knew, didn't have a cat. Once, when she asked Miss Smith why she was buying cat food, Miss Smith said it was for her kitty. Clemmy was at Smith Pond day and night all winter and never saw a cat. She had been in Miss Smith's house several times and there was no cat, no cat smell, no cat hairs, no kitty litter. Clemmy asked again about the cat, and Miss Smith had just said, "She's out now, dear." But the girl knew that wasn't true.

Curious, Clemmy peeked into the groundskeeper's cabin and saw a row of clean, washed and empty cat food cans. She mentioned it to Gabriel, and he put two and two together straightaway. His supply of drugs was given to him in a grocery bag, each ounce camouflaged inside a cleaned-out cat food can, its lid resealed with transparent tape. Gabriel told Clemmy what he suspected, but he did not tell her he was one of Rey Hermanas' teenage dealers.

A short time before Clemmy was lured out onto the thin ice, she told Rey Hermanas she knew what he was doing with the cat food cans. She told him because he wouldn't watch her skate one afternoon when she wanted him to, and she got mad. He left her and she skated anyway, alone. The next day she regretted snapping and apologized. Rey said it was forgotten. But it wasn't, of course. Rey ran to his mastermind, Miss Smith. And Martha Smith went out that day and bought a cat to cover her cat food buying and began to plot the murder of little Clemmy, the sooner the better.

And now we know how to fit in our *means*:

Miss Smith tells Rey to weaken a portion of the pond ice near its center. "Crack it with a hammer," she says, "before first light." Then she tells him to slip into Clemmy's house, steal Clemmy's cat, put it to sleep with drugs, and sling the animal out where the ice is weakest.

## Opportunity

And now our *opportunity*:

Before school the next day, as usual, Clemmy comes to practice. Gabriel is with her. She sees her cat, Double Axel, thinks the cat is injured, and without thinking skates out to rescue it. The ice breaks, and Clemmy sinks into deep icy water.

Gabriel yells and darts after her.

He is in his school shoes, hightop sneakers, and he slides out more than walks. Leaning over the broken edges of ice he sticks his hand down. The water is numbingly cold; Clemmy doesn't surface. Again, Gabriel screams for help. Miss Smith appears at a window. Gabriel sees the woman there and dives in after Clemmy.

But the pond is deep and Clemmy's body has been pulled to the bottom by the weight of her skates. And the water and her struggles have moved her several feet beyond where the ice is broken. Clemmy's body is not directly under the ice hole.

Gabriel swims down to the pond bottom. The water under the ice is dark and heart-stoppingly cold. He does his best, he searches desperately. But he is no fine swimmer. And then, in the icy murk, he touches the soaked fur of the dead cat.

This terrifies him. He pushes back to the surface, gasping for breath. He is so chilled he cannot feel his legs beneath him. He tries to haul himself up and out, but the ice is jagged-edged and breaks away under his hands and burns his fingers. He cannot get a grip. He dives again and can't even find the bottom this time. He is terror-stricken. Up again, he finds himself under the shroud of ice. He slams against it with his palms and can't break through. Frantic, he whirls and churns—he needs to breathe. He sees, through dim water, the lighted place where the ice is broken through and a new sun shines weakly in. He gets to the opening with his lungs swelling like ice packs. He breaks the surface, exhausted. He lays back his head. . . .

Okay. We've got the how and why, along with the who, what, and where. We're almost out of the woods. But let's go on, and finish Gabriel's reaction.

When Gabriel regains consciousness in the hospital, he does not remember anything that happened. To him, that day did not exist. He is touted as a hero, Miss Martha Smith is a hero too—she looked out and saw the two caps, remember, and called the police. But Gabriel knows he is no hero, he is a failure. Clemmy is gone. He could have, he should have, saved her, and he didn't.

Do you see how, one thing at a time, you lace your plot together? It takes some time and effort, but it makes a miniature model of your mystery-to-be, and you write better because of it.

It may be you won't use everything you plot in. You might change things as you go along. But with your model carefully built and solidly standing, you'll be able to move step by step through your mystery knowing the way. If you change nothing from the outline, you'll get home well. And that's what we're after.

- Always, we want to get home well.
- We start. We build slowly, taking our time, one item, one thread, one specific consideration at a time. We correct, we adjust. We leave out incidentals unless we think of one so fine we're afraid we'll lose it if we don't sew it in right then. We smooth, we take a look at what we've got as we go. We find where things work in

easily, we spot the difficulties. We fix them immediately. We don't pass up a knot intending to untangle it later. Line by line, we plot our mystery through to the resolution and the final scene.

# 4. ATMOSPHERE, VOICE, AND POINT OF VIEW

When we talk about *integrity* in a creative work, we mean everything fits appropriately and seems to belong. You know, a stick figure of a representative human being has a head, two arms, two legs, and a trunk. There's no "wrong move," and things are in their proper place. So it will be with your novel. The style of the work will fit the kind of mystery it is, and the murder that's committed, and the characters who are the suspects, the victims, hero, and heroine.

## Atmosphere, the Mood of the Mystery

You can have many different scenes, characters, and actions, but the integrity of the whole piece will come, mostly, from the atmosphere which, in each scene, should contribute to and work toward the overall effect. So you want your atmosphere appropriate, immediate and long-lived. The atmosphere of your mystery will be its *mood*, which can be light or dark or any shade between. You want it in your first paragraph, your first line. You want it from your first word through your last.

&#8226;&#8226; The *atmosphere* of your mystery is the envelope it comes in. It's the first thing the reader sees, the first thing he feels, and the last thing he remembers.

Writers worry about their atmosphere and they are right to. Proper atmosphere makes the difference, all other things being equal, between an ordinary mystery and a good one.

You want your mystery to have a *mysterious* air.

&#8226;&#8226; Atmosphere begins with the first word and ends with the last. In between there is a story, and after, there is a *resonance*. The

35

resonance and your story are what your readers will remember. They'll remember both.

## Voice, Really, Is Tone

Before you write your first line—the famous opening line, which I'll come to—you want to have an idea of the novel's *voice*. Ah, there I've said it, the thing that seems to *really* bother the first-time mystery novelist.

Almost every beginner is scared of *voice*. Don't be. Voice is simply the *tone*, and tone sets the atmosphere. Your novel has to stay in tone the way a singer has to stay in pitch. It's not hard, but do be aware of your tone. Hear it as you write. That way you'll keep to it.

Let's take the time-honored example of the beautiful female corpse stretched out on the library carpet. The tone in which you write this fact varies with what you, the author, want to make of it.

Your tone can be almost neutrally objective: "The body lay on the rose-flowered carpet. It was fragile and white and splashed with red."

Or the tone could be poetical, though poetry in mystery is not in fashion. Still, why not? "Fragile and white and splashed with red, a body on a rose-flowered carpet lay."

There could be a masculine sensibility: "The body lay naked on the carpet. Caucasian, blonde, mid-twenties, splattered with red. Fragile. The carpet had roses in it. Rex Tuff, private eye, crouched over her. The roses smelled of dust."

Or, written in masculine first person: "She was naked, and she was sprawled out before me on the library floor. I dropped on my knees beside her. There were roses in the carpet, but all I smelled was dust. She looked fragile, twisted that way, and so pale. Her breasts and her belly were splashed with red."

Of first person from a feminine point of view: "The body was naked, fragile and pale in the moonlight from the curtainless window. It lay before John's desk on my favorite flowered Aubusson carpet. She looked like a long-stemmed lily, stretched out like that, tossed among too many roses which had stained her a too-black red."

You choose. You can do it any number of ways. Do it the way you want to, the way that seems natural, the way that *fits*. The voice will come, you'll hear it as you write, and write on, and your confidence will grow. Voice, really, is *tone*.

In each of the above examples, see how the story changes? The tone begins to shape the story as it goes. In the first example, the body itself is emphasized. In the second, there's the sense of a lovely young woman doomed in a beautiful environment. And in the third, it's the poetic sense of how fragile life is, how precious and how brief.

- •◆ Voice is an artistic choice.

## Point of View

Closely allied to voice is point of view. There are, I suppose, several different choices in point of view a writer could make to tell any story, but rarely more than one good one.

- •◆ And that one good point of view will be the one in which you, as creator, think of the story, develop it, and plot it out.

For example, let's say you get a splendid idea for a story: A murderer thinks he has killed the woman he meant to, but he mistakenly kills a different one, and that mistake is not discovered until the intended victim returns to the scene of the crime. Innocently unknowing, there she gives an alibi and protection to the guilty person, thereby presenting the murderer with another, surer chance to try to kill her.

This is the bare-bones idea behind Vera Caspary's classic *Laura*. To make such an implausible scenario work, and work masterfully, requires deft plotting and a special point of view.

Let's examine our possible choices here, and then I'll tell you how Ms. Caspary brilliantly solved her point of view problem. I hope you'll see, as we look at the different possibilities, how only one choice was best, and that the best point of view choice was implicit in the story to be told.

## Three Point of View Categories

We have three categories of point of view: singular first person only, singular third person only, or multiple point of view, either first or third person.

### First Person Singular
If we choose first person singular, which person should be the narrator? If we choose the murderer, the reader will know who dunit right out of the

box, and we don't want that; the punch of the murderer's identity at the end will help this mystery's impact. To tell the entire story out of the murderer's mouth and try to keep the narrator-as-murderer unguessed by the reader would not allow the what-actually-happened actions of the other characters to be presented as fact. We want a factual unfolding of the plot to make this story as enthralling as it has every right to be. Choosing the murderer as narrator cripples the telling, so nix to that.

The intended victim, the heroine Laura in this case, won't work either, because Laura must, for a crucial space of time, be unknowing of her intended fate. She must also be unknowing of what happened in her apartment the night she loaned it to her girlfriend and went off to the country to get away by herself and think out her future in solitude.

The police detective on the case (in *Laura* he is the hero) can unfold the story as it happens, all right, but he can't give the character Laura authenticity as a person. The story told from his viewpoint can't really tell us why she did what she did—saying she would be at home, then letting a girfriend stay in her place while she went off on her own without telling anyone what she was up to. For *Laura* as a mystery novel to rise to the high status in its genre that it has, it is necessary for the reader to believe Laura is a woman worth loving and well worth a proud man's hating the loss of—hating to the point of murder, even. For *Laura* to really succeed, the reader must fall in love with the character Laura as the detective does, and the reader will only do that if he or she knows the character is worthy of infatuation.

So, maybe use the police detective's point of view? No, you decide. Much of the poignancy in the novel is that the cynical detective finally is able to fall in love for real, and the object of his love is (he thinks) a dead woman. And part of the enjoyment for the reader comes from the knowledge that Laura is not really dead, that the detective's love for Laura is not completely hopeless. You don't want to lose that aspect of the book. Nope, the detective won't do.

Since these three characters are the principal ones, the remaining choice is "the disinterested spectator," which we can't consider as a choice in this plot, because it involves its characters' private moments and secret thoughts.

So, a first-person-only point of view won't hold the story you want to tell.

### Third Person Singular

Now we turn to third person singular, or what is known as narrative voice. This might work, you think. You could differentiate your chapters according to which character moves each subsequent action and plot development. Why, then, do we hesitate and not plump for third person singular point of view and get on with the novel? Because if we do, we will have to disguise in our narration certain clues to the murderer's identity until the end, and then have to fall back on that old-fashioned scene of explanation where what was not shown at the time needs a final, wordy revealing. And such chapters tend to weaken the impact of the final moment of climax and resolution.

So while we could tell the story of *Laura* in third person singular voice, we would give ourselves problems of technique we'd prefer to avoid. No, the story would be better if more intimate, if it was built, piece by piece, from the limited point of view of each of the characters involved.

### Multiple Voice

It must be multiple voice, then, mustn't it? Separate voices advance the action and reader-knowledge as the story unfolds. And the multiple voices must be personal, so the reader can add what one character knows to what another is able to tell. That way clues can, through the different characters' knowledge of this and ignorance of that, be revealed as needed—dropped in cleanly one at a time—or withheld until the writer wants to expose them.

And that's what Vera Caspary did. She used her multiple voice point of view in the first person and divided her mystery into sections. First one character opened the story and told it up to a point. Then the next took his moment and advanced the mystery to a certain stage, and then the next, and so on. In this way, the reader learned the suspects and the intended victim personally, good traits and bad. And the reader absorbed a rather complicated story structure with ease, and loved every moment of it.

If you can't find an old copy of *Laura*, which is now out of print, try to see the Gene Tierney movie sometime on TV.

## Choosing Between First and Third Person

Your decision to write your mystery in the first person or the third depends on the atmosphere you wish to project and the type of scenes you plan to dramatize.

First person is more intimate and lets the reader know the narrator's point of view very well. First person scenes can be easier to write in that they limit the author's scope, since scenes written in first person can be seen only from the narrator's viewpoint. Of course, you can vary the voice by allowing someone else to impart information—in a letter, a journal, or in dialogue, for example. But told in conversation, first person limits the sense of action and lessens a reader's feeling of being present on the scene. And if it's clear that the narrator is telling about an event that is over, a mystery that has been solved, there tends to be a "past" sense to first person that limits the reader's excitement. It's clear that the narrator has survived somehow, and the villain has been thwarted. No matter how riveting at the time, somehow something that's over and done with isn't as interesting as the exciting things to come.

An advantage of first person is that if you as author don't know the name of, say, an object on a boat, you can make your narrator someone who doesn't know it either. Or if you're writing about what you know well, you can make your narrator an authority and show off your expertise lightly.

Many first-class mysteries have been written in the first person. Raymond Chandler used it and so did Dashiell Hammett. Agatha Christie used it sometimes. Dick Francis uses it most of the time. And so can you.

### Comparing First and Third Person

➤ Ultimately the point of view you use depends upon the story you want to tell and the dramatic effects you're after.

Here's a short example of a scene written first in first person and then in third person singular. The tone will differ and, more importantly, the story will too.

>    *The first time I met Johnny he was robbing a bank—robbing me, really, because I was the teller.*
>    *He was handsome, that I noticed right away, even before he pushed the note toward me and showed me his gun. He was even grinning, and his teeth were nice, straight and even and white as my stepmother's curtains.*
>    *"Oh, hi," I said as he stepped up to my window, and the bank got*

brighter, you know what I mean? That's when he pushed the note at me.

I looked at it and it said only one word: QUIET. So I looked back at him then and he had the gun out, its muzzle pointing right at my heart. The gun was hidden in a black wool scarf he'd wrapped around his hand, easy-like, as though he'd just pulled it off now he was out of the cold.

"Empty your cash drawer and be quick and you won't get hurt," he said.

I'm smart so I got the message right away, and I wondered if he'd get mine. "A guy like you needs a girl like me," I said, and then I opened my cash drawer and began counting out my twenties, a pretty pile.

I could just feel the heat of him, his black eyes boring into my red hair. "What time do you get off?" he said, and it just thrilled me to hear it. His voice was different already, warmer, like I'd just made a new friend.

"Ten minutes to lunchtime," I said and kept my head down, thumbing down the twenties one by one.

"You fooling me?" Oh, even from the first I loved to hear Johnny talk.

I looked at him then and smiled my best and pushed over the twenties, all stacked neat, and shook my head no with my heart as big in my eyes as I could get it.

"Oh jeez," he said, and flipped an end of the scarf over to completely cover the gun. "I'll meet you on the corner."

I tore up his note as he backed off, and then I said, real professional, "You're forgetting your withdrawal, sir."

He just looked so beautiful picking up that $440. Happy, you know, like a man who's just splat fallen into true love. . . .

Now we'll write this same scene in the third person. See how the tone of it changes, and the effect:

The first time Martha Galt met Johnny Ryder was in the bank where she worked. She'd just been promoted to teller and he was just out on parole after serving eighteen months of a two-to-four for assault with intent to rob.

Johnny had a car waiting on the corner with his friend Vester behind the wheel, and the car had a full tank of gas and all of Johnny's and Vester's possessions, which weren't much. Johnny meant to start his life over, and this out-of-the-way branch of the People's Savings and Loan seemed to him a place to start.

He'd practiced his routine so he knew what to do. There wasn't another customer in sight when he went in, but he took his time ambling up to the first deposit window, pulling off his scarf and wadding it into his deep coat pocket around the gun inside there, as though hurry was the farthest thing from his mind.

And then he pulled out the scarf with the gun enclosed in his right hand, and held the note he'd written out earlier in his left. He tried to look timid and friendly, as though he might need help, and then he stepped up to the window marked "1" and grinned for all he was worth at the girl behind.

She gave him back a smile that stopped his heart.

She gave him a smile that said she'd like to know him a whole lot better than she did. And her voice when she said, "Oh hi," sounded like a marriage proposal.

But Johnny meant to have his way, and girls had been kind to him before, so he kept his mind on business and set his right hand on the counter to position the gun the way he wanted and shoved over the note to get on with his future.

The redhead looked at the note and then looked at him as though he'd suddenly made her very happy, which maybe he had.

Johnny kept his concentration, though, and eased away a corner of the scarf so she could see the muzzle of the gun. "Empty your cash drawer and be quick and you won't get hurt," he said.

And then the girl — well, she was a woman, really, a young woman with a pert face and sly green eyes and god-made strawberry hair — said, "A guy like you needs a girl like me," just as conversational as Johnny would have been if the roles had been reversed. And she opened her drawer with opportunity shining in her eyes, and hauled out a stack of twenties and began to count them out as though Johnny were entitled to them by simply asking. Her fingers were quick and pretty, ringless, with seashell-pink nails.

Johnny couldn't help himself. "What time do you get off?" he *said, his mind almost, but not quite, rejecting what was happening to him.*

*"Ten minutes to lunchtime," the siren said. And then she looked at him with everything she had, which let him know she was his for the asking if he only dared ask.*

*A man dreams of such a woman all his life and rarely finds her; Johnny knew that. But hey, he couldn't believe his luck. "You foolin' me?" he said.*

*She shoved the stack of twenties his way in answer. And a good answer it was.*

*"Oh jeez," Johnny said and covered up his gun, for the robbery could wait if she were real. "I'll meet you on the corner."*

*And then the woman of his dreams said in a just-right, high-toned voice, "You're forgetting your withdrawal, sir," while her seashell-pink fingers tore up the note he'd passed.*

*And so Johnny stepped back up and took the money with a smile that let Martha know she'd have a different future after all, for she could see that he, too, had just splat fallen into true love. . . .*

Notice the differences between these two passages. In the passage told from Martha's point of view, for example, the reader is more likely to feel sympathetic to Martha than in the second; on the other hand, we can really only guess at Johnny's thoughts and motivations. In the second example, we get Johnny's thoughts but not Martha's—for all we know, Martha might be planning to alert the police to her rendezvous at the corner with Johnny. The use of the third person omniscient narrator also allows the author to add some information about Johnny that couldn't be included naturally if the scene were in first person: In the middle of robbing a bank, Johnny would be unlikely to think "I want to start my life over by robbing this bank, having just gotten out on parole after serving eighteen months in prison." He already knows this—he doesn't have to go over it in his mind. The reader doesn't know this yet, though; these facts really do need to be included.

Writing third person is harder initially. In third person the narrative voice itself becomes, in a way, a character. It's called "the omniscient voice," and it isn't supposed to have biases or personal thoughts. The omniscient voice is a neutral presenter, a device to set down the story which seeks to make itself forgotten by the reader, letting the reader experience the story and its revelations for himself. But because no writer is omniscient, an author's sensibilities are revealed through the narration, there's no getting away from that. The choice of words, the kind of sentence structure, the adjectives, the verbs, *the style*, all reveal the author behind the narration. Still, the author in omniscient voice must be in control. The author tries not to obviously prejudice the reader one way or another.

Third person narration gives you more options than first person. You can be anywhere, see what you want, ignore what you don't. In third person, the narrator is never tired or beat up and put upon, or swayed by circumstance. In omniscient voice you can leap from character to character, country to country, instantaneously. End a chapter in an attic in Maine, open the next on a mountain in Tibet. You can write a book with more breadth, but not necessarily one with more depth.

### Multiple Viewpoint

Multiple viewpoint is not third person narration, not omniscient voice. Multiple viewpoint uses plural "I"'s or, if written in third person, takes only the point of view of whichever specific character the author wants to use, in any particular scene.

Multiple viewpoint, as used in Vera Caspary's *Laura*, in first person is tricky. It's a writer's gimmick that, when it succeeds, can lead to a *tour de force*. But when it doesn't it tires the reader and tends to "dis-involve" him. The reader tends to listen, in multiple viewpoint, rather than emotionally identify or engage.

## Writing Your Opening Line

Now let's get over the hump of your opening line.

Mickey Spillane once said that the first page sells a mystery novel and the last page sells the next one. I think he is pretty much right in that. He may have been talking from the standpoint of selling to a publisher or a reader, but it doesn't matter which, because it's true in both cases. And since any writer who wants to write one mystery wants to write more, and since from your very first book you begin either amassing or losing readership, we are right to care about our first page, our first paragraph, our opening sentence.

Probably because opening sentences always mean much more than they say—opening sentences, as we've seen, set up *tone*, establish style, display the door through which the reader is invited to enter—and because they are short, compared to the whole novel, aficionados, critics, reviewers, and just plain fans like to remember them (if they're memorable) and quote them. In general, first sentences even more than last ones get more attention in a novel than any other.

In nonfiction, the first sentence is called "the hook." Writing an article on the true-life drowning of Clemmy Chance, say, or a travel piece on the tourist attractions of the little town of Land's Rest, the author knows he has to get the bored-and-looking-to-be-amused reader interested right away. In the newspaper business, a reporter who can write fast and facile "hooks" soon gets a byline, a raise, and a bigger traveling allowance.

In fiction it's a little different, but only a little.

Trying to sell a reader on having a skate on Smith Pond, the nonfiction writer might start off something like:

> *Whatever it is you're looking for in a Saturday skate—clean, thick ice, long banked curves, a pleasant tree-scaped view, uncrowded ice lanes—Smith Pond has it, all day long and all for free.*

But I'd never even think, nor would you, of starting a mystery that way.

Still, though, you want to hook your reader into reading past your first line, especially if that reader is standing in a bookstore looking over books to buy. And to do that, you want a good opening line.

●◆ But remember, no opening line is perfect. *Good* is good enough.

Let's see:

> *It was not till the beginning of September that Ashenden, a writer by profession, who had been abroad at the outbreak of the war, managed to get back to England.*
>
> *Ashenden: The British Agent*, by W. Somerset Maugham

> *It was about eleven o'clock in the morning, mid October, with the sun not shining and a look of hard wet rain in the clearness of the foothills.*
>
> *The Big Sleep*, by Raymond Chandler

In the offices of the Homicide Bureau of the Detective Division of the New York Police Department, on the third floor of the police headquarters building in Centre Street, there is a large steel filing cabinet; and within it, among thousands of others of its kind, there reposes a small green index card on which is typed: "ODELL, MARGARET. 184 West 71st Street. Sept. 10. Murder: strangled about 11 p.m. Apartment ransacked. Jewelry stolen. Body found by Amy Gibson, maid."

The "Canary" Murder Case, by S. S. Van Dine

I was in the Tupinamba having a bizcocho and coffee when this girl came in.

Serenade, by James M. Cain

Mrs. Ferrars died on the night of the 16th-17th September—a Thursday.

The Murder of Roger Ackroyd, by Agatha Christie

When Lovable Lou LaMont, rookie quarterback of the High Mountains Climbers, was killed on the football field on the Colossus Complex, nobody realized what was happening.

Sports Freak, by Shannon OCork

I returned from the city about three o'clock that May afternoon pretty well disgusted with life.

The Thirty-Nine Steps, by John Buchan

The last day of pretty sixteen-year-old Sally Anders' life began much as any other.

A Death in a Town, by Hillary Waugh

*Last night I dreamt I went to Manderley again.*

*Rebecca*, by Daphne du Maurier

*"What in the world, Wimsey, are you doing in this Morgue?" demanded Captain Fentiman, flinging aside the* Evening Banner *with the air of a man released from an irksome duty.*

The Unpleasantness at the Bellona Club, *by Dorothy Sayers*

*On the morning of Bernie Pryde's death — or it may have been the morning after, since Bernie died at his own convenience, nor did he think the estimated time of his departure worth recording — Cordelia was caught in a breakdown of the Bakerloo Line outside Lambeth North and was half an hour late at the office.*

*An Unsuitable Job for a Woman*, by P. D. James

*A Frenchman named Chamfort, who should have known better, once said that chance was a nickname for Providence.*

*A Coffin for Dimitrios*, by Eric Ambler

*The train tore along with an angry, irregular rhythm.*

*Strangers on a Train*, by Patricia Highsmith

Enough. Here's the thing. They are all good sentences and they all pull you to read more. But by themselves, they're only sentences. They begin a tone, they place a setting, they suggest a certain kind of personality. For these sentences to measure up, they need a novel behind them.

- ●◆ Start your story. *Do not worry about your first sentence, almost anything will do.* So forget immortality.
- ●◆ Start your story where it starts, and bang on.

And about last lines?

- ●◆ Stop your story where it ends. No flourishes, no swell of trumpets, unless that's been a part of your style and you need such curtain closings.
- ●◆ Last lines, to be effective, need a whole novel behind them to be appreciated. Last lines are like the vibration of a chord in music.

Well struck, they linger longer in memory than in the ear.

●◆ Don't worry about your last line. It'll be there waiting for you when you get to it, I promise.

# 5. HEROES. . .

## The Hero/Heroine: Series Character versus One-Shot Mack/Maxine

**O**ne of the things you hear in mystery writing circles is that, in general, novels with a series character sell better than novels with a one-timer.

I want to give you as much truth as I can. So let me caution you that in bits of conventional wisdom like this about the publishing world and the book buyer, it's right sometimes or right mostly or right in the *usual* sense. And so, then, it's nearly as often wrong.

But here's the idea:

*If* you want to write a traditional mystery—that is, a "genre" mystery with a crime and suspects and a hero who solves it (I'm going to use hero in a neutral sense, male or female)—

And *if* you plan to break no new ground, meaning that you intend to adhere to the customs of that kind of mystery, you're not going to write a thousand-page saga or reinvent the puzzle, or write with such majesty that you will win the Nobel Prize for Literature with your first bounce out of the box—

And *if* you have a particular venue that appeals to you which you would like to mine, a territory you want to make your own beyond one book, such as Raymond Chandler's Los Angeles, or Dick Francis' horse-racing scene, or Tony Hillerman's world of the American Indian—

And *if* your writing style is not yet developed to the point where you think you can achieve national best-sellerdom on the strength of your first effort—

And *if* you want to enhance your chances to get your first mystery published, albeit the occasional awkwardness and its rudimentary finesse—

- Then, yes, go for a series.
- At least, give yourself the option of starring your hero again.

You can always not follow up if the hero doesn't catch on. Or, if you outgrow the hero and his milieu two or three novels down the line, by that time you'll be a working mystery author with a track record, and your opportunities will have expanded.

## The Problem with Series Characters

Here's the downside. Arthur Conan Doyle grew to hate his immortal creation, Sherlock Holmes, and his telltale companion, Watson. Finally, Sir Arthur *tried* to kill Holmes off at the Reichenbach Falls in Switzerland, only to have to bring him back. The public cried loud and long for more Sherlock Holmes stories, and Sir Arthur was not able to gain a readership for his more "serious" novels. So in time he caved in and brought the master back. And even now, years after Doyle's death, there are pastiches of Sherlock Holmes, innovations and tired copies, and continual new adventures by other writers, all eager to dip into the still undepleted golden coffers that open to the sound of "Sherlock." And, by the way, you too can dip into those coffers, if you are so inclined. The copyrights on Sherlock Holmes have expired. Today, the great man is anybody's meat, and the international public's fascination with Doyle's immortal character is undimmed.

Dorothy Sayers and Agatha Christie are famous for lamenting how tired they were of their respective successful creations (Lord Peter Wimsey in the first case, Hercule Poirot in the second). Nevertheless, in the interests of capitalism, both mistresses of the mystery endured their fatigue and carried their heroes on to further triumphs. On the other hand, Dame Agatha loved her Miss Jane Marple and bitterly resented M. Poirot's claim as prima donna, with readers, of the Christie canon.

Honestly. This problem should happen to you.

Harry Kemelman found a way around it. His series hero, Rabbi David Small, begun in *Friday the Rabbi Slept Late*, gave him an out. After the seven days of the week had been written in as many novels, Mr. Kemelman was home free, his series completed. No reader hungry for more Rabbi Small could reasonably expect more. After all, there are only seven days in a week. But note this too: Have you heard of Harry Kemelman lately? Has he ceased to write . . . or only to sell his latest efforts in the market-place? A clever series character creator, he wrote himself out of his series. He doesn't have to carry the rabbi on through the other twenty-three, twenty-four days of a month unless he wants to. (After a lengthy hiatus, the *Rabbi* is back in '89, with a no-limit title *One Fine Day the Rabbi Bought a Cross*.)

Lawrence Sanders did much the same thing with his series of the seven deadly sins. Sue Grafton has set herself a harder task. Her series hero, Kinsey Milhone, starts with *A Is for Alibi*. So that leaves twenty-five more cases for her before Ms. Grafton is through.

And now let me tell you about Don Pendleton. In 1969 he wrote a kind of "Mickey Spillane mystery," *War Against the Mafia*, and introduced a one-man vigilante posse called Mack Bolan. To make an understatement, the Pendleton mystery was a hit and his hero became a star. Pendleton coined his own catchphrase for the genre, "action-adventure." Other au-thors, seeing Mr. Pendleton's success, followed in his wake. There was so much demand from the public for more Mack Bolan that Mr. Pendleton had to farm his novels out. At this writing there are 120 *Mack Bolan, the Executioner* titles, and two other entire series, *Able Team* and *Phoenix Force*, based on characters who first appeared in Mack Bolan books. There are now even "SuperBolans," novels of longer length, and more novels in each series coming this year and the next and the next. . . . Don Pendleton is now an industry unto himself. His publisher, Gold Eagle Books, said that as of August 1988, there were over 125 million Mack Bolan novels in print, and more coming. If this kind of boom-bam mystery appeals to you, you can read more about it than I know in Writer's Digest Books' *How to Write Action/Adventure Novels*.

But let me tell you this, too. You want to write a mystery and you want to survive to write another, but you won't want to spend your life and talent drawing just one hero over and over again in different circum-stances. You're going to want to grow as a writer, and that means that different styles of mysteries and different heroes will siren-call to you. So if you're locked into a successful series you mean to continue to write yourself, and you want to try a different kind of mystery, the only way to do that is by pseudonym.

That is, my god, if you've got the stamina. Some writers do, they sure do. Erle Stanley Gardner wrote a novel a week, and took weekends off to write others under a pseudonym. Well, writers like that are a different kind of horse and long may they race. They not only write facilely and fast, they write well and entertainingly. They give you a good read, every time, for your dollar.

## How to Get Your Hero in a Whole Lot of Trouble

Now that you've decided that your principal character will at least have the option of being a series hero/heroine, and you've got your plot outlined and your characters named, and you know you're going to tell your story along the line of the apparent plot and let the real one break through from time to time, and you've written beyond that opening line, what do you do now?

You get your hero in a whole lot of trouble.

And how do you do that?

Start your main character off amid problems of his own. When the novel opens, things are not rosy in the hero's immediate situation.

Take Aurora Gorham, for instance. She's a young widow with a problem stepchild who almost drowned and has been hospitalized, traumatized by the loss of his only friend, and is hostile toward his stepmother. Aurora wants to earn Gabriel's love, and she wonders, *fears* that Gabriel may have been responsible for little Clemmy's drowning.

Hoping that isn't true, but ready to face it if it is, Aurora sets herself looking into why Clemmy Chance's cat was stranded out on the thin ice of Smith Pond. As she does, she will be misunderstood by Clementine Chance's father, her maybe love interest. She will be ordered off the Smith property or—let's make it worse—chased out onto the pond herself by the property caretaker, sexy, mysterious Rey Hermanas. When he doesn't follow her out, she wonders what he knows about the ice that she doesn't. And maybe she finds something out there, floating up in the hole where the ice broke. . . .

And then let's say that Miss Smith, our villain, decides to frame Aurora as the head drug dealer of Land's Rest. After all, Aurora, once a nurse, is now at the hospital tending to Gabriel eight hours out of every twenty-four. She has access to doctors' prescription pads. She would know how to write a proper prescription. With some sly maneuvering, she would even have access now, within the hospital, to a supply. So let's have, as soon as Aurora begins nursing her stepson, the theft of a large amount of morphine from the hospital's stores found in Aurora's knitting bag, which she brought to the hospital to keep herself busy while she watched over Gabriel, who is still in a coma.

Here's the idea the way I first heard it:

You put your main character out on a cliff edge. You have him fall over, hanging on by his fingertips. He's tired, and the wind is high. Below, waiting for him, are wild water and circling sharks, anxious for his hide. Then the bit of earth he's holding onto starts to slip. And then, as he struggles, trying to scramble to safety, the villain looms over him and stomps down, chuckling, on the hero's fingers. One hand falls away. Helpless. Useless. The villain leaps to crunch the other hand and the bit of earth on the edge of the cliff gives way. The villain falls upon the hero. The hero lets go his faltering grip. . . . *Oh boy.*

The idea is that, while *really* in your story, you move your hero toward happiness and solution, you *apparently* shove him closer and surely to his doom. The turnaround from doom to triumph is the climax of your mystery. Good ultimately wins out, but only at the last nanosecond.

●◆ So don't be quick to give your principal character rest. Keep him uneasy, anxious, harried, *in constant jeopardy.*

Now along this dangerous road you're winding, your hero has his successes —

●◆ But you use each success to foster another difficulty.

Let's say that during the commotion when the morphine is uncovered in Aurora's knitting bag in Gabriel's hospital room, the boy wakes and wants to know what's going on. The head nurse leaves with the morphine to report Aurora to the authorities. Aurora tells Gabriel that morphine, stolen from the hospital supply, has been found among her things. Gabriel says, "Not yours. Mine. I took it and put it in the grocery bag. I think the cat ate it by mistake." Then he lapses back into unconsciousness. Aurora alone hears him say this, but makes no sense of it at the time. She is only relieved that Gabriel has passed a certain critical point. His momentary coming to consciousness indicates that he may, if he is lucky, pull through without brain damage. So even though Aurora has been unjustly accused — perhaps intentionally framed — she still has the little victory of Gabriel recovering, and she has been given a new clue to think about: what Gabriel just said.

The cat on the lake, the cans of cat food Miss Martha Smith was shoplifting from the supermarket, the town up in arms over the drug dealer who is haunting the high school—these are all problems for Aurora to solve. And now she needs to clear herself of suspicion in the drug theft, so she has much to think about.

Then Clemmy's father comes to see how Gabriel is doing, and Aurora meets him. Aurora's hours with Gabriel are over for the day. On impulse she invites Donovan Chance to have dinner with her. He says yes. Almost as soon as he does, Aurora begins to fear *him*, suspect *him*. He was too quick to agree, she thinks. He wants to get her alone, perhaps plant more drugs in her house . . . but she takes him home with her. She asks him, over the wine, about Clemmy's cat. Still bereft at the loss of his only daughter, Donovan Chance is not at his best. He drinks too much, too quickly. Then, in the bathroom down the hall from the kitchen, the bathroom Gabriel normally uses as it is just off his room, Clemmy's father finds some of Gabriel's drugs and thinks Aurora is, indeed, involved in dealing.

He leaves before dinner abruptly, rudely. But he tells Aurora before he goes that Clemmy's cat was in her first heat. Before he left for his classes, earlier than Clemmy did that fatal morning, he shut the cat in the bathroom and told his daughter to be careful not to let it out. So Aurora wonders how it was that the cat did get out, and understands a little better why it was so important for Clemmy to get her kitty off that ice and safely home. Clemmy didn't want her cat to have kittens too early. Double Axel was barely more than a kitten herself.

And then Aurora, wondering why Donovan Chance walked out on her, goes, musingly, into Gabriel's bathroom and finds a bit of cocaine powder spilled out into the tub. She immediately thinks it is *Clemmy's father* who's a user, Clemmy's father who's to blame. . . .

So that's the way. You zigzag from one problem to another, gradually increasing the pressure of the danger as, overall, things get worse and worse while, under all, things get better and better. Pretty soon, there is only the ultimate scene of dangerous confrontation to play out. When that is done, all the other "under" things have been pretty much straightened out so that, the murderer exposed and caught, the happy ending is quickly possible. The quicker the better, so as to end the novel with impact.

- Step by step, scene by scene, then, you build toward the ultimate confrontation, twisting your way along, not going straightaway.
- You *spiral*, like the threads on a screw. Swinging around one twist you end up a little higher, a little tighter, a little closer to the edge.

# 6. . . . AND MURDERERS

The thing that worried me most about my first mystery was whether I, knowing who the murderer was, would somehow give the game away to the reader and ruin his fun.

That first time, halfway through, I realized I had. So I changed the murderer in my mind, which meant changing the real story under the apparent one, which meant replotting and starting the novel over.

## The Murderer and How to Hide Him/Her

The mistake I made was that my murderer, rather than my heroine, was the book's most interesting character. Plotting the novel through the first time, my author interest was in the murderer and the real story. I held him vividly in my mind, his devious motivations, his clever opportunity. I oriented the apparent story around the real one, and as a result the real one showed through in my first draft the way a floor does under varnish.

The solution? Flop the emphasis; reverse it. Wrap the real story around the apparent one.

- Concentrate your novel on the *apparent plot*. After all, that's your story. Make the most interesting character your hero or the victim or the one who might be the next victim, not the murderer.

Agatha Christie, one of the most clever plotters there ever was, had this trick down pat. (She was made a Dame of the British Empire, she was so good at her job.) *The Murder of Roger Ackroyd* was her first *tour de force* and her first international hit. In that novel her narrator turns out to be the murderer. This was a famous first. Much hullabaloo issued from critics and fellow writers when *Ackroyd* came out: Did Christie "cheat" the reader or didn't she?

No, she didn't. She used ambiguity in some of the sentences surely, but she did not play foul. She fooled us all, brilliantly. The narration is written as though it were a journal and her Dr. Sheppard, as she says in her autobiography, was the kind of killer who prided himself on never telling a lie.

See what she did? She incorporated a character trait—in this instance the doctor's pride in not lying to his journal (which is the novel)—to hide the doctor himself as the murderer. What Dr. Sheppard did was to carefully record his time with Mr. Ackroyd and their final conversation. And then he slithers over the actual murder with the ambiguous words, "It was just on ten minutes to nine when I left him, the letter still unread." There is a silent gap of ten minutes to be filled, but what fine reader grasps the significance of that?

●◆ You too can hide your murderer through his characteristics and hide your tricks in characters' flaws or foibles.

Using the hypothetical mystery we worked on earlier, the murderer, Miss Martha Smith, outwardly a sexually uninteresting spinster, must be shown to be *really* a woman of passion and daring to make her villainy, when it is revealed, acceptable to the reader.

To the town of Land's Rest, she is one of its most virtuous citizens, a model of good form and sterling character. We have already portrayed her as intelligent; we've made her a fine mathematics teacher. Let's say that she is caught, later in the day after little Clemmy drowns, shoplifting those cat food cans. Our heroine, Aurora Gorham, is shopping hurriedly so she can run to the hospital to stay with Gabriel. Anxious, she spins around a corner and bumps her shopping cart into Miss Smith, who is behind a tall display of pet toys, slipping cat food tins under her roomy sable coat. Aurora doesn't do anything about it, doesn't even let Miss Smith know that she saw. Preoccupied, she forgets the incident almost as soon as it happens.

But when Miss Smith is checking out, she is caught again, this time by the checkout girl.

Miss Smith dithers and blushes. The store manager is called, she vouches for Miss Smith's probity. Miss Smith pays for the cans, shaking her head at herself. All the excitement of the little girl drowning, she says, has addled her mind.

In a subsequent scene, pages and incidents later, two elderly shoppers whisper to each other about Miss Smith getting caught stealing. One of them is the checkout girl's aunt; the checkout girl told her about it. Both the shoppers will be of the same generation as Miss Smith, they'll talk about the vagaries of age, and one of them will say something like, "I remember when Martha and I were young. One time she stole socks for the boy she was in love with. Took them right out of her father's drawer."

"How romantic," the other one says.

"Yes," says the first. "She was fourteen and quite mad for the boy. But he was poor, you see, and they were rich, and, well, she always was generous to those less fortunate than herself."

"But *socks*," wonders the first. "Why not dollars out of her father's wallet?"

"That would have been too much, I'm sure. I remember those socks, though. He wore them all winter. They were bright crimson."

"Poor Martha," sighs the second. "And she's still, all these years, so generous to the children."

"Even rich, life isn't perfect," nods the first. "Ah, here's that new color bleach I told you about. On special."

And the little scene is over, misdirected at the end, throwing the characters' view of Miss Smith over her true one.

Something like that. It's not too much. It's just a stroke, something small from childhood spurred by passion as evidenced by the color red, something in the maiden lady's character which is even likeable and forgivable. The reader feels sympathy for the elderly woman who never, the reader thinks at this point, consummated a love affair.

Does this work? Like steak on charcoal, if you do the same for your other characters. If you give each of them a little particularity of character that could be construed as a flaw, you hide the murderer's black heart and still play fair.

●◆ If you show a little imperfection in all your characters, you hide the imperfection you need for your murderer in plain sight. If you can show the murderer's imperfection sympathetically, so much the better. No one likes to think the worst of someone he likes.

- But don't concentrate on your murderer.
- Concentrate on your hero/heroine.
- Concentrate your novel on the mystery to be solved, not the solution.
- Concentrate on the problems your hero has working his way toward that solution.
- Concentrate on the victim. Why him or her? What, of all the things he was and did, brought him to such an end?

As the apparent story unwinds, spiraling to climax, the real story bleeds through.

# 7. SUSPECTS, VICTIMS, AND RED HERRINGS, TOO

Before we begin this chapter, a caveat:

What the fiction writer cannot do is invade the privacy of actual others, spill their secrets, broadcast their woes, identify their foibles, smear them to their detriment while they live, make them recognizable to their friends and peers.

There are, sensibly, laws against such things. Libel is the defamation of a living person. In fiction, if you tell "Tom's story," for instance, his other acquaintances should not be able to identify your boss, your brother, or your neighbor across the fence as "poor Tom." What might happen (and does) is that people you never dreamed of will come up to you and say, "I recognized myself in your book." You'll be astonished. I think authors' friends go looking for themselves.

In my first novel there was a character named Amy Bland. I chose all the names from people I did not know. After *Sports Freak* appeared, a woman I had met after the manuscript had been written and sold but not yet published got mad at me. She thought I had mean-spiritedly defined her personality; her name, sigh, was Amy. When I told her that I had named that character knowing no Amy at the time, she didn't believe me.

So in a way you can't win with these things. There will always be someone who thinks he sees himself in your work. Is it his ego, his insecurity, or your shortsightedness? I don't know. If and when this happens to you, just take it on the chin, tell the person he's mistaken, and let it go. But do *try* to name your characters so that others in your immediate field of acquaintance don't see a connection between an actual Amy and a made-up Amy Bland. Also, if you do want to use a real person's story or a fact therefrom, change your character radically from the original.

Here is a story which may or may not be true, but I learned from it. A writer wrote a novel using the personality and professional specialty of a doctor she had taken treatment under. To write the novel, she made the real thin man fictitiously fat. He was clean shaven in real life; she gave him, in her fiction, a Freud-like black beard. When the doctor sued, he showed up in court thirty pounds over his weight when she had known him and sporting a full-faced, trim black beard. And so the poor novelist lost her case.

Now what she should have done, literary lawyers say, was to lose that doctor's identity in a gender change, an age change, and all possible particulars of personality. If the novelist's doctor had been a glamorous woman now — case dismissed. So change the gender, change the age, and alter all physical resemblances. From blond to bald, from brunette to fiery redhead, from Anglo-Saxon lineage to Hispanic or Chinese, from an assertive personality to a sly, subtle one. Then you will hold your novel in your hands guilt and lawsuit free, and hopefully keep your friends.

## Minor Characters

And now back to craft. We've already figured out that we don't want any more characters than we can effectively use; too many ingredients make a stew of the pie, to mangle an old saw. Still, though, we want as many characters as the story takes.

So let's move from the less important characters to the more so, from the simple to the complex.

- ❖ Some minor characters need be used only once to further your plot, set an atmosphere, turn a single scene, or act as a representative of a kind. These characters can be named or not, according to your preference.

For instance, let's say your mystery will be about a woman, a good cook who plans to kill her husband. But though she tries and tries, she doesn't succeed. Along the way, though, she kills others, testing her "samples." Finally she will be caught, either trapped for the murder of one of her "guinea pigs" or, in a case of ironic justice, mistakenly test-sampled to death herself. Perhaps she offers herself in a weight-reducing experiment. But you open the novel with her getting away with her virgin misadventure. The first victim is important to the story, then, only to advance your plot:

> *The old man was feeling particularly well. The kind woman had just given him a meat pie, a whole wedge, still warm and fresh-smelling. Tucking it slyly under his ratty coat, he limped industriously to a warehouse he knew where no one ever went, where he wouldn't be bothered and none of the others would take his prize from him.*
>
> *It wasn't far, and he was hungry. He was almost blind, and whiskey had rotted much of his brain, so he did not notice the man in the orange hard hat stooped over the rectangular canister with a T-shaped handle. And the construction worker, carefully readying himself for the dynamite blast, did not notice the stumbling slip of a man.*
>
> *Inside, in a corner beside a long-gone window where he could see the sky, the old man sat himself down with a grunt, and smiled at his good fortune. With shaking dirty fingers he began to eat. The pie was juicy and sweet with meat. But there was a bitterness in it, too. Perhaps spices? He couldn't remember spices anymore. He sighed, wiped his mouth on the cuff of his coat and ate more. It's the whiskey, he thought. Whiskey's ruined everything for me . . . And then he closed his eyes and tried to identify the bitter spice. Nutmeg-like, it was. He remembered nutmeg, from the orphanage at Christmastime. Or maybe almonds. . . . His head drifted back against the wall. The sun shone on his rheumy eyes. There was spittle on his lips as he died, and a vague, nostalgic smile.*
>
> *Some minutes later the blast went off and tumbled a part of the warehouse. No one noticed the old man was gone.*

That's all. A simple little scene, the character never mentioned again in your story, but your novel is off and running, the character performing his function for you, doing all you want of him.

You could name the old man if you wanted to. Change the opening just a little:

> *He was born Henry Hilton, a fine name, he thought. But all his life people had called him Bud. Today he was feeling particularly well. . . .*

And then, in the last line: *No one noticed that Henry Hilton was gone.*

Maybe giving him a name gives him more reader sympathy, a little more dimension as a person. With his fine name there's a sense of chances lost, of a lifetime of failure, a sense of human regret. But really, that's a little thing. Either way won't make or break your mystery.

So that's one way a minor character functions, as a plot device. And when you use a character this way, be respectful of him.

●◆ Give the least of your characters *dignity* if you can. If even the least have the reader's sympathy, the reader will like what he reads, will be drawn emotionally into your story. There will be that illusive, all-important *resonance* I spoke about before. The reader will begin to *feel*, and it is in feeling that reader identification starts, and echoes.

Minor characters can be used, throughout your story, as "bridges," or transitions, too. As a bridge, a character functions as a connecting link from one action or episode to another. For instance, in an earlier chapter I talked about the two elderly lady shoppers, representatives of the townsfolk of Land's Rest and their attitudes. Some minor characters used this way are classic. In an old English suspense movie, *Night Train*, directed by Carol Reed, there are two tourists, typical middling-age English gents who, in the midst of Nazi intrigue in a little overnight hotel, go through the entire turmoil never knowing what's going on and worried only about the British cricket scores. Not only are they dandy comic relief, irresistibly lovable and dim, but they break up the intense moments of epic complication so that the viewer can catch his breath and more easily follow the twistings of the plot. Alfred Hitchcock stole these characters for his *The Lady Vanishes*. He swiped them right away and had a hit with his "fellow travelers" as well.

Agatha Christie is a master of bridge characters. And, of course, Dr. Watson carries this bridge role for Sherlock Holmes, as well as being his narrator.

You may not need a character to bridge events, to misunderstand them, or tell them from a different point of view to the main character's. But if you do, take care of him. Give him his dignity. Make him very human in his one-dimensionality. Emphasize his foibles and universal humanity.

●◆ But scoot him through his assigned tasks. Don't linger on the likes of him. Keep your story at a run.

## Major Characters and Details

The other characters in your mystery, the more actively participating ones, will all have greater or lesser importance to the main plot. They're treated differently. They get a three-dimensional quality. The problem with them is that you want to make them alive (at least until you kill them), but you don't want them to slow down your momentum.

What to do?

●◆ Define by detail. One or two or three will do.

Just a moment. I knew I'd have to get to the description-versus-action argument, so I might as well have at it right now.

Yes, description is all right in a mystery novel. I mean, come on, how can you tell any kind of story without some kind of description? What are words for, anyway?

This is what words are for: They convey information *and* association. *Association*: How one thinks, today, of a word; how it ordinarily relates to things in our social discourse. What it usually *signifies*.

*Pink.*

What do you think of? Lemonade or tulle. Something feminine or pretty, something mild and sweet. Or, in the case of pink elephants, something silly and highly improbable, a harmless (and hopefully temporary) apparition of a drug-distorted mind. *Pink*, as a color, has *certain associations*.

As a writer of suspense and mystery, you have a choice. You can use descriptive words in their usual associative way if you want, or you can *flop* them, reverse the association, and make one particular thing into its opposite, for sinister effect.

Take a pink pill, for instance. . . . No, better let an unsuspecting victim-to-be take it.

Or how about a pink window shade drawn down in the daylight, flounced up in the night? What couldn't such a shade reveal? . . . Let's look.

Or what if there's a pink intestine where smooth stomach ought to be? . . . Oh, dear.

Or a pink garter belt about a cleric's throat? . . .

Or, regarding a character, what if one of your suspects always wears pink as her most becoming color except on certain days, and on those days a series of murders are committed around the school where she teaches? The reader might wonder what, if anything, "the pink connection" was, and you, as author, will make it mean something important. Perhaps Miss Pinkly doesn't wear it on days she must meet her brother, who controls the family finances, because she knows Tom cannot stand pink and goes "stingy" on her when she wears it. Or perhaps the pretty creature is, indeed, a Jekyll-Hyde type, and when the evil Hyde is in control of her personality, unconsciously she chooses a different signature color to identify her persona. Or, again, perhaps the true murderer pathologically sees Miss Pinkly as his signaler to act, and when, just for a change, she omits her pink pin or sweater or jacket or such, he takes this as a devil's command to strike. However you work in "the pink connection," you make it matter to the story; pink can be a saving characteristic or a damning one, depending on how you shade it in your tale.

Or let's take another example. What's the most likeable attribute a person in real life could have? How about generosity? If you want, you could write a mystery of such a "Santa Claus" character who is, by virtue of that one attribute, victim, suspect, or murderer. If a victim, perhaps someone he benefited wanted more of Santa's largesse and thought to get it via Mr. Claus, will. If Santa is suspect, perhaps the victim was a recent recipient of Santa's bounty and then, as Santa was heard to say, wasn't properly appreciative enough. And if Santa is a murderer, perhaps the generous one gave his gifts in order to control or possess another person who would not let himself be so captured, and so roused Mr. Claus to a killing rage.

The point is that, in a mystery especially, attributes of character or descriptions of a thing may be used at first to disguise and then to zero in on the mystery to be solved.

When modern experts of the mystery advise keeping description in your novel to a minimum, what they really mean is *eliminate all description of no purpose*. We're not going to write meaningless description. Everything's going to count. Everything means *something* and has its purpose. If it doesn't, and it crept in, on rewrite we strike it out.

So we have to describe. And what we'll do is use the description to reveal or conceal, to give motive to one suspect, opportunity to another, means to a third. We'll set up vulnerabilities and strengths, we'll *define* our characters by the way they decorate their rooms or wear their hair and by their gestures, by what they do well and what they do poorly. That way it's not description, it's *revelation*. And it's vital.

●◆ So we define by detail.

Here, in a couple of lines, is not only a whole description of a certain kind of woman and her way of life through how she looks, but how she was expected to look and didn't, and what that meant to her daughter-in-law to be.

"Audrey had envisioned Dolly Dowd as small and mewling, an old cat still kittenish and devious; an aging sexpot, with bleached hair thinning at the crown and wrinkles between her breasts. But this woman before her was plump enough to be firm-skinned at fifty, and though she would not see thirty again, she was not yet the other side of forty. This woman was still able to bear children, in the prime of her life. This woman looked as though she knew how to get a day's work done and how to laugh while she did it. This woman could get a man to scrub the wood oil out from under his fingernails and make him like it. . . . This woman was dangerous." (*Turning Point*, by Shannon OCork.)

Here's another.

" 'Now there's a bright boy,' said Detective Florio. He squeezed himself into a chrome-frame, yellow canvas director's chair. The chair squeaked under the load and sank about six inches. He offered over the box of hot dogs. I shook my head no. He picked up the first, cold one. 'So talk, Baldwin,' he said, and filled his mouth." (*Hell Bent for Heaven*, by Shannon OCork.)

Here, the chair of the artistic person who's just left ("the bright boy" Detective Florio referred to) serves to define an unartistic man who sits in it. But the detective is a smart man, and he's confident and hard. And he's a man of no pretension who eats when he's hungry and who almost always is.

In the second example, the defining of the detective takes place as the story moves along. The first is from a novel of romantic suspense where moods and impressions and misapprehensions are stressed and kept heightened. The second is a mystery with a female sports photographer as amateur detective with a murder to solve. For different kinds of novels, you do it different ways.

- But what you do is the same. You bring a character alive, you give him dimension, by particularizing him *within a scene's environment*.
- Define *in* action, not by it.

A character is defined not in *that* he acts, but by *how* and what the action is. A character is shown to be what he is by his responses to others' actions, too, and by how his own acts are received and perceived by others. And you can delineate what he thinks of himself during the action.

Look at this sentence: *Janet ran for her life.*

Not so good, is it?

"For her life" defines Janet as running as fast she can, I suppose, but it has nothing, really, to reveal about Janet. After all, if a man with an ax in attack position ran at you screaming "Banzai!" or saying anything unpleasant at all, wouldn't you run? Bet your booties! So would we all. Nope, this won't do.

We try: *Terrified, Janet ran.*

Ummm, I still don't like it as it lays. True, we now know something about Janet, but it's so vague it's almost a cliché, a real yawn.

*Janet ran, lifting her heavy folds of skirt above skinny knees which, since she had entered the nunnery thirty years ago, had not been so exposed to day's bright light; she prayed, as she fled, for God to forgive her.*

This one I'll buy. This one tells me all I'll probably ever need to know about Janet. And I am filled with sympathy for her. I hope she gets away, but I have my doubts.

- We don't need to tell everything there is to tell in one sentence. As we move our character along, we add one item this time, another the next, in context.

## Creating "Tags" for Your Characters

If you have a lot of characters who are more or less alike in age, social status, and situation, one way to introduce the whole and yet keep each suspect/victim straight in your mind and the reader's, is to *tag* each character with a physical or verbal mannerism or an overriding interest in something that the other characters don't share.

●◆ Give each character a "uniqueness," which, for a while, you keep on the character like an invisible hat.

Say your murder mystery takes place at an exclusive resort. It's a class reunion. They're alone at the inn. Each classmate will take a turn cooking a meal for everyone and, generally, they're all supposed to be roughing it. But things get messy from the first night, and then downright fatal.

You could make a list of your characters and tag them as the list is made, even if you change a tag or two later. Maybe do it something like this:

*Elmtree High School Class of 1965*

*Nancy Foxx.* Voted Most Popular. Divorced, well-off, a Manhattan interior decorator of business offices. Chic and thin, she's always eating like a horse. Except she didn't touch the Melba mousse that night, even though she supplied the recipe.

*Alex Bailey.* Class Valedictorian and voted Most Likely to Succeed. He says he's never even been in a kitchen since he left his mother's house, and he likes to talk about the grand restaurants he's eaten in around the world. Carries a current *Michelin Guide* in his blazer pocket and wants to buy dinner for everyone at the restaurant down the road when it's his turn to cook. But he knows what a "fish poacher" looks like. He goes right to it in the inn's overstocked supply room, and his *sauce hollandaise* on the asparagus is perfection.

*Helen Price.* She married classmate Tommy Price, all the girls' heart-throb. Everyone wondered why, because Helen was so ordinary. She still is; same old Helen. Even her *steak tartare* is bland.

*Tommy Price.* Handsome and charming then, a jock. He's a big business executive now, disciplined, preoccupied and controlled. He used to have a "crush" on Phyllis Deeter, the class "bad girl." Now he acts as though he can't remember who she is, but nobody believes that.

*Phyllis Deeter.* She used to wear fluffy tight sweaters and short straight skirts. Now she seems to be down on her luck. Her once-black hair is laced with gray and it's straggly, and her clothes are shapeless and cheap. She never married, she says, and has no job. She claims she's a beach-bum; her figure is still the best in the class. She rooms with Nancy Foxx, who notices at once that all Phyllis' lingerie, all the stuff the others don't see, is more expensive than Nancy's own. And she's the only one who arrived by private plane. And she made the Melba mousse.

*Carolyn Cook.* Class reporter, and the one who organized the reunion "cook-in." Carolyn always knew everybody's business. Even in the old days she had hidden cameras at all the parties and sneaky tape recorders in the cafeteria. She'd hate it that she's the first to fall and so will never know whodunit.

You get the idea.

Now, taking those tags, you hang them on each character when he's introduced and carry one along for a while, until the readers know everybody well. Then you need only refer to a tag when you want to.

And then, as soon as you write:

"A shadow trembled on the stairs where the banister turned to meet the attic, a shadow oddly reminiscent of Elmtree High. There, again, were young curves molded in fuzzy mohair above the streamlined length of naked legs. . ." the reader knows who the shadow is meant to suggest.

➽ If you can, make the tags figure in the plot, either as red herrings or real clues. It's good to do that; it gives your mystery a professional shine.

Some authors of mysteries like to make their victims people worth killing, and some like to make them innocent and undeserving of their fate. Either way works, but the trend today is to make victims likeable and even the villains seemingly so. Have it your own way. The genre is flexible, and what was hot twenty years ago can flame today. There is room at the top, and room in the middle, for all kinds, all ways.

➽ This is important: The mystery novel thrives on individualism.

While I'm for respecting traditions and knowing the work that has gone before, I'm also for *individual style.* Find yours. Hone it. Put your name on it. In time you may find you've started a tradition all your own.

Turning your characters into suspects is easy. Remember *means, motive,* and *opportunity*?

The *means* is how the murder was done. Or murders.

The *motive* is why.

And the *opportunity* is *the ability to have been where it happened when it did, or to be able to cause it from a distance.*

You can turn each surviving character into a suspect by giving each a motive, a means, or an opportunity. Not all to all, nor none to none. Space things out, show a little *probability* for this one, a little for that. Leave some things for several characters-now-suspects unexplained, let there be a few *ambiguous possibilities* for others.

I'll show you. We'll look back on our character tag-descriptions and see what we have.

Nancy Foxx. Here's a grown woman, divorced, who when she was young, was sought after by all the boys of her class of Elmtree High and maybe all the boys in her neighborhood, and maybe every boy she ever met. Still attractive, she could have come to this reunion to sift through her past for Husband No. 2. Or is it No. 3? . . . Or was she ever really married to that man she disparagingly refers to as "Handsome"? None of her classmates ever saw him, after all. And she has no children and she retained her maiden name. And hers was the recipe that concocted the dessert that killed nosy Carolyn Cook.

Come to think of it, didn't Carolyn dish up some dirt about Nancy in senior year? Something about a final term paper Nancy paid Carolyn to write for her? Of course, that was long ago, but Nancy was kicked out of the honor society because of it, lost a scholarship to Smith, and ended up having to go to State U, for heaven's sake. And maybe that loss changed Nancy's life, ruined Nancy's life, in her opinion. . . .

Like that.

Give some characters obvious *possible motives*. You can give a motive anyone would want to kill for, such as the victim killed off all your family and is now tracking you. Or you can present a motive that is "iffy," one maybe you and I wouldn't kill for, but that we accept as reasonable that some people would react violently to, even after years, if need be. Then give a few of the others possible "hidden" motives, surrounded by maybes.

Take Alex Bailey. He professed too loudly his ignorance of cooking; that *Michelin Guide* to the world's great restaurants and all that, what flimflam. Alex is a fast-food junkie. His idea of fine cuisine (as far as the others remember) was a pizza with the works. But he prepared a sublime meal. And he pointedly refused to make the dessert, so dull little Helen Price made that. "Anything to avoid a scene," she said. Well, what's Alex's problem? Carolyn Cook was nothing to him, *was she*? . . .

Another:

Tommy Price and Carolyn Cook sat by themselves when she ate the

Melba mousse, out on the edge of the terrace overlooking the sea. Their backs were pointedly to the others, still inside at the dining table. Tommy had the opportunity then, and *maybe* a motive, because Carolyn was pregnant, and Helen admits to everyone that Tommy is not faithful to his marriage vows.

## Red Herrings

If you give one suspect no motive, no means, and no opportunity, every reader will suspect him. This comes from the old-school trick of making the least likely the one who, genius-like, thought up and brought off the perfect crime — or would have except for the intervention of the real genius, the hero master detective.

But you can use this reader tendency to your advantage if you want.

- Give one character ostensibly no motive, no means, and no opportunity and make him innocent. You can rest assured that this character, whatever use you put him to, will be watched every breath and move by the reader. This character can be one of your red herrings.

Red herrings are so-called (I think) because there are no red herrings. However, my *Random House Dictionary of the English Language*, unabridged 1966 edition, gives as its first definition under red herring: A smoked herring. So maybe there are some red herrings, but they're disguised.

- Anyway, what we mean by red herrings in mystery writing is *false clues*. They fit the *apparent* story, they seem to be relevant, they seem to lead the reader toward the solution, but, in the *real* story, they lead to wrong paths and erroneous conclusions.

Red herrings may be more fun for you, the writer, than for the audience, but they are an accepted, an integral, part of the game, so use them for all they're worth and enjoy them. Readers will be disappointed if you don't.

- Through your red herrings you'll be able to make your innocent (and so essentially less important) characters as vivid and interesting, even more so, than your villain, whom you're neglecting and leaving a little musty and dusty so his true colors won't show.

One example of a red herring is in the last chapter, where I showed you Aurora Gorham finding the cocaine dust on the rim of her bathtub after Donovan Chance had been in the bathroom. She thinks he spilled it, using it in her house on the sly. Suddenly, then, his character changes in her eyes. But you, the reader, know this isn't so, because I told you the cocaine was Gabriel's stash. Mr. Chance only found it and put it back, but he didn't clean away all the traces. He thinks maybe *her*; she thinks maybe *him*. That's one kind of red herring, the kind the reader sees through but a character doesn't.

The classic red herring is when the reader doesn't know. The reader has to try to see through the author's intent, has to try to reconstruct the real story from the apparent parts he's been given. When Miss Martha Smith is caught shoplifting those cat food cans, the readers wonder if this is a red herring or if the old lady might be, somehow, involved.

You know that episode is not a red herring because, truly, Martha Smith is not only involved, she's the villain. The big red herring about Martha Smith was at the beginning of the novel when she acted the good citizen and called police emergency to report two children drowning in Smith Pond.

Daphne du Maurier's *Rebecca* is full of beautiful red herrings. The heroine, the second Mrs. de Winter, finds so many evidences of her husband's late first wife that *seem* to show Maxim's adoration of her. Rebecca's bedroom at Manderley, for instance, is not to be used by the second wife. It is left as it was on Rebecca's last night, the most beautiful bedroom in the house, kept fresh-flowered and groomed and untouched, as though it is his memorial to his first wife. And he travels with a book of poems Rebecca gave him and inscribed to "Max" with blackest ink. And he asks his second wife to call him "Maxim," which is much less tender than the fond nickname Max, and he replies, when the second Mrs. de Winter asks, that Rebecca was the most beautiful woman he has ever seen. The accumulation of details is very convincing, the reader sees and hears and finds along with the new bride — and interprets as the bride interprets, *incorrectly*. *Rebecca* is a shining piece of work, as perfect in its execution as a mystery novel gets. And in red herrings, I think it has never been surpassed.

Here are some smaller red herrings. The whole mystery may not turn on them, but they're tasty reading.

In *The Maltese Falcon* by Dashiell Hammett, Sam Spade's affair with Iva Archer, the wife of his murdered partner Miles Archer. While on the one hand, Mr. Spade's vulnerability to a pretty woman is true and helps define for the reader the kind of man Sam Spade is, the fact of the affair has nothing whatever to do with the death of his partner, although the police seem to think it does and for a while the reader, new to this hero, isn't *sure*. And that's what you want of a red herring: *misdirected suspicion*.

S. S. Van Dine liked red herrings too. In his *The Greene Murder Case*, the apparent story concerns itself with trying to protect one of the members of the Greene household, when better attention might be made to protecting anyone else. For the "intended victim," who, though wounded, survives what is thought to be a double murder attempt in which only her sister dies, turns out to be systematically killing off all the rest of her family, or mightily trying to. So while the police hover over the seeming chick in the henhouse, they are really enabling the fox within to proceed with her bloody work.

Well, I'm sorry to spoil your mystery reading.

But here's another point about red herrings that you want to note and remember:

- If they are scattered through the middle of the novel, while the complications and the hard struggle of ferreting out what really happened is going on, they can really lift a scene, spice up a minor character, add suspense and help your novel gain momentum and focus, all while you work through complication to complication.

Red herrings, nicely done, hold the reader with intense interest because the reader, trying to see through the *apparent* to the *real*, grabs onto any arresting fact, pouncing with satisfaction. And a frequently pouncing reader is an engrossed and happy one. He's hooked and running with you. And that is what his entertainment—and your mystery—is all about.

- To keep your reader *gripped*, serve him up, every so often, a crisp, well done, bright red herring.

# 8. PACE

**P**ace is important. It's one of the first things editors look for in a coming writer. It's more important than plot. Editors, if they like you, can repair your plot—they're good at ideas. Pace is more important than background or the ability to craft memorable characters, and even writing skill. Some editors think pace can't be taught, that you either have it, in which case *great*, or you don't, end of story.

Well, editors are wrong on that. Those without a natural sense of pace can learn it. *But if you don't have it, editors probably won't be interested in you until you do.* When certain professionals and teachers and critics of fiction writing talk about born writers, often they mean a writer with an innate sense of pace, the forward progression of a story. For forward progression, you, a mystery writer, think "spiral." Some writers do seem to have a better sense of how to twist the screw up and around than others.

I'll let you in on the secrets of pace, but first let me tell you this: Today, in the writing marketplace, pace is one of the golden words. And since editors are going to be looking at your writing pace, you want them to like yours. Be conscious of your pace. More than any other attribute of your mystery, good pace can make the difference between a sale and an almost sale.

First, what pace is not.

- Pace is *not* just running from incident to incident. Too bad; if that's all there was, it would be easier.
- One writer's flat-out run is another writer's dogtrot. Pace is not speed.

Robert Ludlum jet-skis. Charlotte MacLeod minces with a lady's tread.

Mary Higgins Clark enjoys a controlled and enviable canter. Gregory Mcdonald skips to his different drum. Robert B. Parker sometimes stops dead and circles. The late John D. MacDonald kept a consistent lope. They're all good writers; they all sell well. They all have *pace*, and each of their paces is different from the others'.

Pushing your story along from this to that to then to so on is only *episodic*; if your way of telling each incident remains at the same emotional level, the entire novel will suffer from sag and dullness. Nothing will stand out, your effects and impacts will be lost. There will be no peaks of intensity which the reader will thrill to; there will be no way to bring the reader down from the dizzying height, to let the emotion subside a little only to build it ever higher to a new taking-in of breath. You will have no quivering, shivering respite when *anything-might-happen-and-something-surely-will* to a surge of *here-it-comes* excitement, to the final, we hope, heart-stopping finale from which the reader cannot rear his captive head.

- Pace is not suspense, though the two, together, make a successful novel even if the plot is pedestrian and the characters less than Dickensian. You can have suspense without pace and pace without suspense, but you don't want to. You want them both and you want them plenty.

What pace is:

Pace is the forward progression of your story at its appropriate rate. Pace allows for anticipatory pauses to shiver and for atmosphere to spellbind and for moments for the reader to identify and empathize with the situation and the characters' troubles. Pace presents the story in its best way.

- Pace is the building of momentum and the sustaining of tension for maximum effect of the climax and the satisfying end.

Pace takes a reader from opening curiosity to an ever-deepening interest, through an emotional involvement to a passionate obsession that is lifted only at the end. Successful pace is demonstrated by a coming-back-to-his-own-world sigh from your reader when he comes to the end of your book. Let a reader regretfully close your mystery, all done, not knowing where the time has gone to. Let him wish, as he closes you down, your next novel were immediately in his hands. Then you will know that you are one of the lucky writers who understands *pace*.

This, when he or she reads you, is what an editor will want to do. This is what you want that editor to do.

Pace hypnotizes, bewitches, won't let the reader go. Pace envelops the reader in desperately wanting to know how the story will all turn out. Your mystery need not run frantically from place to place, from murder to near-murder and around again till there are none. But it needs *grip*. It needs to involve the reader in the fate of the principal characters as they wind in the labyrinth struggling to get out, while, as they circle ever closer to the precious exit, unbeknownst to them, before it the slavering monster waits. Somehow the reader is halfway through before he knows it. He leaves your mystery only if he must. He has to turn one more page, read one more chapter; he is *dying* to know what will happen next.

- *What will happen next*: Your reader wanting to know that is what pace is.

How do we get it?

We make the reader *care*. We make the reader interested in the outcome as though it's his head on the line, his health, wealth, and happiness, his hide in danger.

And how do we do that?

We stir him emotionally. First we catch him up in the *situation*; that interests his mind. Then we touch his heart or his fears or his dreams. We want him to identify with the hero or heroine, we want the reader to *vicariously* transfer his own private emotion to the fate of the principals in our story. And we do that by pace.

In a way, it's like love. First stirred, everything about the loved one matters. Pace never lets the reader reflect on his infatuation. It blinds his disbelief and keeps the enchantment up by not losing the story in irrelevancies.

Pace takes a situation and a character and mixes them together and moves them all the way to plot's end. Along the way it doesn't lose its hold. It runs the story *its proper way*, no sidetracking, inexorable as the ocean's tide. Sometimes it's quick, sometimes it's slow, but it's always, ever, *flowing toward its end*. There's no dead end and backup, no letting go, no digressions, no detours.

I'll try to show in the following two examples how pace can go slack in a scene, and how to catch yourself when it does.

Here's an example of slack pace. See as you go how it doesn't really pick up and catch fire:

It's a big step to go from dreaming of killing off your rival to actually doing so. Why, it had been easy, Angela thought, figuring out how she would kill Marilyn Baxter if Marilyn ever made the mistake of coming into the Hat's Off! Beauty Shop to get her hair permed. Well, now Angela thought of it, working on Edith Edderly's impossibly thin hair, it hadn't been that easy figuring out just how. No, Angela had mulled over the possibilities for days and never would have come up with "the perfect solution" if Hugo, who had the chair beside her, hadn't told her about poor Mrs. Potts who would never be the same again after the hair dryer shorted while she was under it the way it did. Poor Mrs. Potts, even if she did get a quarter of a million dollars in an insurance settlement, would never be pretty again. And if she'd had just a little more cotton wrapping around her head, Hugo said, they'd never have been able to get Mrs. Potts out from under the dryer in time to save her life.

So it just seemed like providence when Hugo quit to go to Florida with Mrs. Potts, as the only hairdresser she trusted to touch her, and then the two new hair dryers Wanda bought for the shop came with safety instructions that showed how, if you weren't careful and left wire a touching wire b, you could kill your customers in three minutes' time.

So Angela experimented at home, just to make her anger at Marilyn Baxter ease, and last night she'd learned how to twist wire a around wire b loose enough in her home hair dryer so that what shouldn't happen to a dog happened to Angela's dolly.

And now, now Hat's Off! was so busy nobody knew what anyone else was doing, Marilyn Baxter had just walked in, and was running her fingers through her long dark hair, showing Wanda how it needed perming to give it volume. . . .

Did you fall asleep? Probably not, as I hope the possibilities of this story caught your interest. But you weren't really riveted, were you? So now I'll try to write the same again with pace, and see how she runs:

*It's a big step to go from dreaming of killing off your rival to actu-*
*ally doing so. Why, it had been easy, Angela thought, figuring out how*
*she would kill Marilyn Baxter if Marilyn ever made the mistake of com-*
*ing into the Hat's Off! Beauty Salon to get her hair permed. Hugo*
*helped. He told her about poor Mrs. Potts, who would never be the same*
*again after the hair dryer shorted while she was under it the way it did.*
*And if Mrs. Potts had had just a little more cotton wrapping around her*
*head, Hugo said, they'd never have been able to pull her out in time to*
*save her life.*

*And when the two new hair dryers Wanda bought arrived with*
*safety instructions that showed how, if you weren't careful and left*
*wire a touching wire b, you could kill a customer in three minutes'*
*time, well, Angela experimented at home. And what happened to her*
*dolly last night shouldn't happen to a dog.*

*And now, hallelujah, Marilyn Baxter had just walked in, running*
*her fingers through her long dark hair, showing Wanda how it needed*
*perming to give it volume. . . .*

This is how you keep the pace: You keep your mystery on track. Whatever
*apparently* is going on, let the *real story* proceed to its conclusion. Don't
lose sight of where you're going and how you're going to get there. Keep
up the integrity of the real story while you dazzle with your apparent one.
Go slack on the apparent story if you want, but not on the real one. Run
the *real* like a tight ribbon through the flounces of your plot.

If the serial murderer is after the lovely redhead, keep him after her,
drawing closer and closer. Let her lock her front door; he'll be climbing the
stairs to the back one. Let her admit her lover for dinner; the serial murderer will deliver the Chinese take-out and case her apartment while she
tips him. Let her call the police about the obscene whispering calls; the
serial murderer will be a telephone technician who knows how to circum-
vent a tracing on the line.

Whatever happens, let it count toward the climax. Whenever the hero
or heroine gains, let the gain profit the end of the story too. Pull your two
ends toward each other constantly, the good end that is the victim trying
to save her life, and the bad end that is the villain seeking to take her life
from her. Everywhere she turns, everything she does, twists her strand by
strand toward the final confrontation.

That's the secret. That's the only trick. Let everything *contribute* to the

Big Moment, the scene for which your mystery was written.

And when that moment has been come to and gotten through, end your work. Your story's over. Think of a zipper. Mesh your real and your apparent story tooth by tooth as the mystery climbs to its end. Finally the two sides meet. Then, snap all closed, and *pop*, you've done it.

# 9. CLUES AND HOW TO HIDE THEM

**M**ore than any other writer, Agatha Christie inspired me to try my hand at a mystery. One summer while I was pegging away at my little pieces and trying to give them away for free—yes, I said *trying*—I read maybe fifty Christie paperbacks. They didn't take long, they read easily, and they were fun. Especially, they were clever and oh, so civilized, I thought; the characters kept such admirable tone. Best of all, as far as I was concerned, Ms. Christie played fair with her clues. After reading one through to the end and going back and reading it again, the clues, I knew then, that counted were set down just as black as they ought to be. Ms. Christie made it seem *so easy*. Why, I can do this, I said. Now, let me see. . . .

Well, you know and I know it isn't all that easy. One of the marks of a master of craft is that the effort and the strain don't show. And Ms. Christie at her best is indeed a master of the mystery.

For grand examples of the master at work, see her *The Mystery of the Blue Train*, where not only the suspects are not who they seem, but neither is the crime, nor the motive behind it. Of course there is her *The Murder of Roger Ackroyd*, elsewhere mentioned. And for sheer trickery, read her *Death on the Nile*, which plays on the truths or lies that lovers tell about each other to other people, and how far into sin true love will go. One of Agatha Christie's great strengths as a mystery writer was the way she was able to take commonplace truths, such as "blood is thicker than water," and make an original, unpretentious, entertaining mystery out of it.

But she can fail badly. *Elephants Can Remember* seems to me one of her worst, and there were others I bought that were so dumb I threw them away, half read, as unworthy of my collection. Most of those were when

Ms. Christie was trying for the international spy thriller; in my opinion, not her playing field. But when the lady was good, she was very, very good. For an at-home course in the craft of the mystery, I recommend reading her.

## The Omitted Clue

One of the most famous clues in mystery literature is the dog in the night that didn't bark, when, if the story that was told of what happened was true, the dog should have. Arthur Conan Doyle's Sherlock Holmes figured out that one. And a good clue it is, because it's one of omission; instead of something dropped in, something is subtly and simply left out. But please be cautious using negative clues. What's not said or done, when revealed, must be something every reader will agree ought, under the circumstances, to have been. And that can be tricky. Consider the woman who doesn't weep when she is told of her husband's sudden death — there could be a hundred explanations and more, many of which might, if you wanted to play it that way, prove her innocence. But how about a baby who doesn't recognize its "mother"? Now the mother has some explaining to do.

## The Clue That Can't Be Found

Another famous clue is the murder weapon that can't be found in Roald Dahl's short story, "Lamb to the Slaughter." In this example of superb mystery-telling, the wife kills her husband with a frozen leg of lamb, then cooks it and serves it up to the unsuspecting quartet of police who investigate so long they miss their dinner hour. After feasting, they sit around the murderer's table wondering what kind of big club must have been used to so fracture a man's head, and never suspect what they've just done. Only the reader — and the happy new widow — know.

## Clues from Real Life

In the true-life tragedy of the kidnapped Lindbergh baby, the lot number of the lumber used to build the ladder became a famous clue. Real-life crimes are a good place to scout for clues, but change them to suit your story. Instead of a maker's mark on lumber, use the price tag of a particular store on a hammer. Or have your detective pause over the special "designer-house" thread on a dropped button. Whatever particularly fits. And then lead or mislead, to satisfy your purpose.

## Hiding Your Clues

Now, looking back, what I think Dame Agatha did best, what I noticed most in her excellence beyond the wonderful twists she gave her plots, was her ability to drop a clue straight as straight and have me miss it. Not all the time. I paid attention as I read. I participated in the mystery and tried to solve it, so sometimes I saw through and even "guessed" the murderer and then mentally patted myself on the back for it. But even when I pointed myself correctly, I never picked up every one of the clues and I never saw all the ways the lady could spin that screw.

Well, no one, probably, ever does pick up all the relevant clues and dismiss all the misdirecting ones in a good mystery. And the answer to why this is, is because clues are easy to hide.

Edgar Allan Poe, who started the modern mystery off, showed us much of the way. In his short story, "The Purloined Letter," a dastardly French diplomat stole a love letter from a member of the French royal family that had been written to a woman he should not have been writing such pretty words to. The diplomat blackmails the crown, threatening to reveal the letter's existence. The prefect of police comes to Dupin for help in getting the letter back, the police having, without the villain's knowledge, searched the diplomat's hotel suite—top to bottom, inside the table legs and all—without success. Promised a reward, with a wave of a superior hand, Auguste Dupin produces the letter and all is well in France.

And how did the brilliant M. Dupin find the precious letter? Knowing what it should look like, he looked for its opposite. Knowing it should be hid, he looked in plain sight. The finely wrought royal letter he sought he found, turned inside out, dirtied and soiled, addressed to the villain himself, and almost torn in half, contemptuously tucked into a card rack hanging from a bulletin board like an old and faded invitation to an unimportant party.

And that is exactly how you do it.

- ●◆ If the clue to be presented is a big one, make it appear small. If the clue is "lost," set it out in plain sight among its like on the buffet. If the clue is pretty, soil it. If the clue is dangerous, sheathe its claws. If the clue is something old, borrowed, and blue, present it new and golden, wrapped in cellophane around its bill of sale.

You know the saying, "Don't judge a book by its cover." Treat your clues the same way. The more "give-the-game-away" the clue is to your mind, the more casually you drop it into its scene. The less telling clues, you trumpet. The reader likes to feel he's picked up something as he reads along, after all. Your detective can blare his or her "aha's" on the little clues and keep superiorly quiet on the more important ones.

Let's say one of your clues to the murder is the murder weapon itself. Let's say that weapon is known to be a heavy, blunt instrument that pounded, fatally and but once, upon the victim's head. Let's say this victim is the lovely blonde we left blood-splashed in the rose-carpeted library of chapter 4. The blood has come from her shattered skull. Now what killed her?

You want the weapon to be an unabridged dictionary of some seven or eight pounds. After all, we're in the library, eh?

To make that dictionary really squash the beautiful Miss X, it would have to be precisely dropped from a great height, maybe forty feet, and the ceiling of the library is twenty. High, but half what's needed. So obviously the murder weapon cannot be *exactly* that dictionary. . . . What to do?

Let's make *two* dictionaries, outwardly alike. One is what it is, Webster's Unabridged, 1933 edition. The other is a facsimile, hollowed out as a concealing place for jewels. Jonathan, who owns the library, is a collector of "British Royalty in America" memorabilia. He owns a ring that had belonged to King George VI, which had been dropped at a hot dog roast given for the monarch by President Franklin Delano Roosevelt during the King's visit to America in the early days of the Second World War. The ring was found by a guest at the party and later sold to the highest bidder, Jonathan himself. Since that stately visit was the first time a king of England stepped foot in America, the ring is a prized possession. Miss X knew about it, knew the ring was housed in the false, concealed-safe dictionary, and had gone into the library to try to steal it, with poor results as far as she was concerned.

But the readers and the hero or heroine on the case don't know about the second, false dictionary yet, nor that the dictionary, its safe-space filled with a block of lead, increases in weight to a lethal thirty pounds. You can fill the bottom shelf of a rack of library books with dictionaries, one of which is the murder weapon, mention the dictionaries as part of the contents of the library, and your readers won't recognize the clue before their eyes.

Fun, huh?

Then you can drop more clues, obvious as all get out, about how Miss X was an elegant society thief who got invited to baronial houses and lifted items of value, and what does that all mean in relation to her murder? The reader doesn't know yet but wants to. The reader feels he is on to something, and he is, and he reads on to find out what. You haven't misled, you've *misdirected*. The reader is going to be concentrating on the valuable *knowns* in Jonathan's library, not the *unknowns*. And a dictionary, while valuable to writers, isn't usually of itself, of high value in a collector's market. You will, of course, make sure that you mention the relative worthlessness of Jonathan's book collection.

➡ So there you are, with clues in sight all over the place, successfully hidden. It takes a little planning (never underestimate the value of planning out your little incidents—you will be well repaid for the time), but the effects can be the making of you, especially if they're amusing and original. The tired and overdone, no matter how cleverly you do it, will not be as much admired as something done for the first time, even inexpertly.

Let's say that, in another instance in another mystery, the hero knows that the murderer he seeks is red-haired. Well, you could have this mystery take place during a Duchess of York look-alike contest, males and females invited to participate. Or you could make the red hair a red herring (which is discussed in chapter 7) by having it be a wig or toupee, or temporarily dyed for the murder occasion, or perhaps even a close-fitting red fox cloche seen in dim light or from far enough away so that the "hatness" of it cannot be distinguished from a head of hair itself. Or you could have your murderer, a born redhead, appear on the scene already dyed a different color, maybe a fine brunette.

So that's the game. Present the clue in altered fashion, looking like what it isn't. And then, tightening the screw, let the toupee slip or the roots show faintly through—on several suspects at once. None of them, by the way, may be the guilty party. No, at denouement, that may turn out to be the *hairdresser* who is gray on top and thin of strand and who keeps her modest glory covered with colorful designer scarves, but who knows how, *in a pinch*, to make her hair as red as pomegranate juice, as red as blood. . . . Clues can be fun.

- ❦ Play fair with your clues, but don't be afraid to disguise them, and disguise them with imagination.
- ❦ Once you have a clue in place, don't dislodge it too quickly.

Some mysteries are built on a two-part plan. One half presents the mystery to be solved and the clues and red herrings; the other half unravels the confusion and presents the solution and the murderer. As simple as this sounds, many classic mysteries work just this way. And those that are a little more subtly built still use the best of this simple two-part plan, so:

- ❦ Don't give away a secret unless an effect can be pulled off by doing so, a sinister, disturbing effect which promises something bigger than itself to result from it.
- ❦ Dropping a clue into the phase-out of a scene is a neat way to end one chapter and gain impetus to begin the next one.

Here's how, in my early days, I ended the second chapter of *End of the Line*:

> *We stayed there in the cockpit, side by side. Shivering, the rest of the ride in. Nobody came out of the cabin. The body of Jeremy Yunker remained disrespectfully uncovered. Smirking in the dark. As though it knew something we didn't.*

My bland little clue here—that the murder victim knew all there was to know about who killed him and why and how, but couldn't tell—isn't much, I grant you, but it suggests, in the smirking, a little of Yunker's bad character. And the swinish disregard several guests on board the fishing boat show for the body in their worry about themselves reveals their selfish innocence.

Ending chapter 7, I gave away why one suspect didn't want to be found and the fact that there were two necklaces, at least, in the mystery. (In fact, there were three, one more than I really needed, but I was trying very hard):

> *"Why's he hiding?" This from Floyd.*
>
> *"Oh," she said brightly. "Gordie's trying to kill him. Gordie says Av stole the Kittridge necklace. Av says he didn't."*
>
> *"The necklace was in the black satchel you put on board the Glaucus," said Floyd.*
>
> *"I know," she said, very small.*
>
> *Floyd looked at me and I looked at Floyd, and we left her. Just like that. Went upstairs, got the box with the necklace in it, got our camera bags, and scooted. Out to the road.*
>
> *Elsie watched us, crouched by the pump. Stroking the fat cat.*

Ah, those were the days. I wrote broken sentences and got away with it. Remember when I said you didn't have to be perfect?

# 10. SUSPENSE AND DIALOGUE

S uppose we're sitting in your kitchen having soup. There's a big log burning easily in your fireplace, your dog is snoozing on a mat before your door, and on your compact disc Artur Rubinstein plays Chopin just on the edge of hearing.

I say to you, "There's a storm on the way."

You look at me as you break a cracker and say complacently, "Oh, that'll be nice. We can watch it from the picture window."

"No, it won't," I say and stare at your hands crushing the cracker into your soup.

Instead of dismissing the subject as you had before, now you're mildly interested. "Why ever not?" you ask and take a spoon of soup.

"I saw a rainspout on the horizon as I pulled in," I say. "Hurricane Davy. The bad one they promised. Remember the warning last night?"

"No," you say. "I didn't listen. Hurricane Davy?"

"Davy Jones," I amend.

You've put your spoon down now. You're looking out the kitchen across the living room to your long window over the sea.

"Where's Tom?" I ask. Mr. Rubinstein precisely strikes a chord.

You glance for reassurance at the soft rise and fall of your dog's sleeping sides.

Tom is your only child. He's seventeen and out on the water for his first solo sail. Inland people, you've just moved to the shore, and Tom never learned to swim. He's gone across the sound to pick up his father and bring him back. You hadn't wanted him to go, but he has gone. "It'll be fun, Mom," he said, and Gregory, your husband, had agreed.

"He's probably on Shelter Island now," you say, your voice distant, your mind far from me, on him. "They'll stay over if there are storm warnings, I'm sure."

"If they hear," I say. And as I say it, together we hear the wind rising, whistling around your chimney corner. In the living room, the fire spits.

"Maybe I'd better call over there," you say and you stand away from the table. The dog wakes at the sound of your chair scraping and whines once and sniffs at the crack along the door.

You try to call the house where your husband was staying but you can't get through. There's only static on the line and a forlorn and lonesome ring.

"Perhaps the storm's hit there," I say.

Out the picture window the sky is suddenly dark. A long finger of lightning stabs down the sky and a great boom of thunder rolls and rolls.

I join you at the window, the soup utterly forgotten now. Not far and advancing, a long gray funnel twists from sea to sky. Around it water stands as walls, then crashes in streaks of foam and builds to walls again, higher, ever higher, fortress-high. Just outside, waves whip upon the rocks. Full of force, they thrash and pound, their crests spittle and rip and cling like claws.

The telephone rings. You leap to it, then put the receiver down without a word replied. "They left an hour ago," you say to me. "They must be right in it."

The sweep of storm advances. The wind screams never-endingly. Chopin cannot be heard. Upstairs a window breaks. *Whoomp!* And a door slams and rain runs in the bedroom. You hear it above you, chattering, pattering, destroying. Your dog is up now and his eyes are fearful. He lifts his nose and howls. Nervous saliva drips from his jowls.

I take up a pair of binoculars and sight through. "I see a boat," I say.

You snatch the glasses from me, press them against the window and try to see for yourself. "Where?" you pant at me. "I can't find it, I can't see *anything*!"

I take the glasses back and search. "It was just heeling over as I spotted it," I say.

"My god," you manage to strangle out your throat. "Please let it not be Tom and Gregory." Unaware of what you're doing, you twist your hands.

"Was the boat named *Peaceful*?" I ask. "I see some broken boards floating, and a piece of bow with that name. And oh my god, there's two bodies, they seem to be lashed together. . . ."

But you have collapsed now; you've been done in by *suspense*.

And that, very simply, is how you create suspense and keep it going.

●◆ First, introduce a menace.

Any menace will do if it's (1) believable in context and (2) well and vividly presented. This is another turn of the same coin that says any plot will do if it's workable. But remember that "workable"; it means what it says. Sure, great is better. But *workable* is good enough.

●◆ Then tell what the menace threatens. Let the menace threaten more than just one thing. What's that saying? *Life and limb . . .?* I like that one. Let what the menace threatens be things the hero and the reader will care about. Then bring the menace *around*. Not *in* yet, but around. Show the beast. Let the dragon flick its tail and maybe bite one peasant and eat one virgin and burn the only bridge off the island with its brimstone tongue.

●◆ Then let the menace, bit by bit, *invade*. Let the hero quiver and worry and tremble. Finally, Johnny- or Joan-come-lately, the hero stops running and begins to resist. Bit by bit, on the other side now, the hero turns and fights back. As she does, she takes a few knocks, loses a few rounds, makes a few mistakes. These setbacks take you through the middle of the book, the opening portion being the introduction of the menace and the hero's lack of acceptance of it or the how-to to fight back. In the middle part of the *pervading suspense*, the menace *seems to be winning*, though the hero is putting up the good fight. Of course, at the end, during the exciting finale and at the very last second, the hero—*hurrah!*—wins out.

●◆ As soon as the hero wins, the suspense is over and so should your mystery be.

●◆ It is on suspense that most first efforts fail.

## Using Dialogue to Build Suspense

Somehow, on first try, with so much to think about, the writer's focus on menace gets diffused. The first-timer trots off happily on chatty dialogue that doesn't contribute toward the spiraling tension of the mystery, or he gets his principals out of the danger he got them into without sufficient time and trouble, or he forgets to pin the menace on the *life and limb* of the hero, or some such other serious letdown. When any of these things happen, a story rambles and the reader yawns.

- •• Good dialogue is one of the best tools you can use for the creation of suspense.
- •• Cultivate the habit of caring about and fussing over your dialogue. Like pace, like atmosphere, like a good "vital idea," crisp, believable dialogue counts mightily toward the overall effect, and, hence, the success of your mystery.

Creating good dialogue is important. To be honest, some writers do dialogue easier than others. Experts say this is a matter of ear. Some writers cruise the streets eavesdropping on snatches of strangers' conversations. (I once overheard the fascinating line: "Well, what did you expect, him tryin' to do it in them fancy shoes!" Oh I could write a book on the suggestions that sentence gives me.) Some writers repeat to themselves a certain expression they notice in an acquaintance's speech patterns. Some writers keep a notebook of bright lines they think up in their tub or bed, and then wait for the chance to dole them out to a character in need. Some writers speak their dialogue aloud as they write it, and if it doesn't sound right hanging there in the air, they rewrite until it does. And this is true too: Most writers sweat over their dialogue, wanting it right, wanting it good, wanting it authentic.

Here are several ways to confess to murder, and the one you choose would depend upon the kind of character you want to say it:

*A mathematician*: "It wasn't murder, gentlemen, it was justifiable self-defense. He sought to kill me, and I, rather elegantly I thought, successfully inverted his equation."

Here, you see, you take some of the jargon of the profession, just a little, because you don't want to confuse your reader with techno-talk he doesn't know, and use it as a way to define your suave numbers man.

*A scorned girlfriend*: "Don't be ridiculous; I didn't kill Herman, he killed himself. And anyway, he deserved it. He demanded the diamond back. I threw it out the window. Don't think I cried when he fell out after it, ha!" This time the character shows hurt and maybe an opportunistic, hard little heart.

90

*A business partner*: "Listen, pally, Herman Strickler knew more ways to red-ink the books than my kid has T-shirts. I had to kill him, can'tcha see, he was ruining the business."

Here, there is an appeal to male bonding through the faulty logic that the business is more important than the man.

*The merry widow*: "Greedy, greedy, greedy, that was Herman. This morning I said to myself, Mattie, you just have to stop him. Why, you'd have done the same thing, Officer. Imagine, not only did he insist on a divorce, he wanted the apartment and the summer house too. Leave me just last year's dresses, I suppose. So I poured all the digitalis into his V-8 juice. Worked like a charm."

And here we have the impulsive, if unrepentant, murderer, who can't—or won't—see what she's done was wrong.

So, dialogue not only conveys information, it establishes character. But now, let's say, you not only want information and character in your dialogue, you also want suspense.

Rewriting our examples, then, we tell less and move the action forward after each tidbit of conversation. I'll take just one, the merry widow, because I like her best:

> Mattie Strickler offered Detective Keen an iced glass of vegetable juice. "Greedy, greedy, greedy, that was Herman," she said, and watched the detective gratefully drink.
>
> "How was that, ma'am?" asked Detective Keen.
>
> Mrs. Strickler sighed. "Well, you know, don't you, Officer, that Herman was absolutely insisting on divorce."
>
> "Yes, ma'am," said Detective Keen, and felt his heart jump. He looked for a place to sit and eased himself down on the candy-striped sofa.
>
> "And he wanted everything," Mattie said, her eyes bright and frightened both. "The apartment here in the city and the summer home. Leave me just last year's dresses, I suppose."
>
> Detective Keen sipped again at the vegetable juice. "Almost seems like this health drink has a kick to it," he said.
>
> "Yes," she said. "It's Herman's. Was Herman's. I made up a pitcher for him. Saturdays, I always do."
>
> "About how you killed him, then, ma'am." Detective Keen drew a dark line on his notepad.

*Mrs. Strickler poured the rest of the juice into the detective's glass, and then sat opposite him and folded her hands. "I said to myself, Mattie, you just have to stop him. Why, you'd have done the same thing, Officer."*

*"I don't think so, ma'am," said Detective Keen, his heart flying in his chest. He took another long swig of the vegetable juice. Mrs. Strickler became instantly two. Sweat beaded on his forehead. He swiped at it with the little cocktail napkin.*

*"So I poured . . ." Mrs. Strickler began, but Detective Keen had it now. He roared up, dripping sweat, and stared at her with unfocused eyes.*

*". . . all the digitalis into his V-8 juice. Worked like a charm."*

*The house, but not Mattie Strickler, trembled as Detective Keen fell.*

●◆ Work on writing good, constant, and building suspense.

Start your suspense wide and then narrow it, narrow it. Squeeze it down, episode by episode, upon your hero or heroine's head. From the threat of a general storm, go to the family dog driven crazy by fear or the relatively small inconvenience of a broken upstairs window. Rain on the floor is no reason to write home, but knowing your entire family is dying before your eyes and you're helpless to prevent it, may be. And the strain of not only losing your family but your just-bought and heavily mortgaged house, and perhaps even your own life and limb. Well, it starts to get to a person after a while. And the straw that breaks the camel's back might be a leak in the roof, absolutely ruining that all-day-in-the-making soup.

At least it should keep your reader awake.

## The Cliff-hanger

The aptly named *cliff-hanger* is a handy writing device that helps keeps the suspense going in one scene if you want to break it off at a particularly harrowing point and jump off, or back, to another place.

Sometimes you want to halt the suspense to bring in another part of the picture. The old bridge-word, "meanwhile," as in "meanwhile back at the ranch" or "the pool" or "the castle dungeon," used to work well until it got overused and tired. Now we have new ways to break away and bridge or go back to another plot thread we left hanging. But whenever we leave in the middle of an unfinished scene, we do it by cliff-hanger.

•• Just leaving off in the middle creates its own cliff-hanger. When in doubt how to do it, remember this. Just stop where you want to, like this:

*Now she was helpless. Leering, he closed upon her.*

End of sentence, end of paragraph, end of chapter, interruption of scene. A successful cliff-hanger.

Another:

> *There was nowhere to go. Before her was only towering, gas-exploding fire, to her right and left crumbling walls of flame. And behind her slithered the creature, filling the hall with his growling underbelly, belching smoke. His scales glowed cauldron-hot, his fangs arrowed toward her. But nowhere was better than the monster's belly; despairing, Allison reached out and embraced the fire.*

Every half-hour TV soap opera has about eight or ten scenes that jump back and forth between each other, and each scene fades out on a cliff-hanger. Some are more, some are less, successful. But you can see cliff-hangers in action, every day if you want, by the dozen.

The least effective cliff-hanger is the unanswered question, either by a character or, in a novel, by the narrator. Someone asks whatever happened to poor Tom. And the other character either turns away or slams out a door or stares bug-eyed or bursts into tears or *does anything* except answer the question. When it's done in narration, there may be three little dots that follow the period at the end of a sentence. . . . Or maybe not.

•• But while questions may be the simplest and least effective, still they work, so don't throw away the thought of using them. And, used once in a while to emphasize a point, they can be all the cliff-hanger you need.

Next-best in the hierarchy of cliff-hangers is the character brooding on something that disturbs him.

Let's say Monica has been getting, over the past week, obscene phone calls from a breathy whisperer. Monica lives alone, leads a predictable, decent life, and can't imagine that the obscene caller knows her. She thinks her number was just randomly dialed. Not too worried, only disgusted and annoyed, she's reported the calls to the telephone company, which will change her number in three days. At the end of this chapter you have Monica almost complacent when her telephone rings again. Soon this nuisance will all be over, she is thinking. She smiles as she picks up her telephone. And then the caller whispers her new number to her and cackles malevolently, and repeats his rude suggestions. Startled, Monica slowly sets down the receiver but hears, as she drops the instrument into its cradle, the caller whisper her name.

Monica is more than upset now. She is afraid. You end the chapter with Monica wondering who he is and what he *really* wants of her and how she is going to escape the caller *now*. So that kind of cliff-hanger works, too, and it has the advantage of *echo*, of resonance, of pulling previous, unconnected incidents together, and of throwing upon the chapters to come the *ominous foreshadow*.

But the best and classic cliff-hanger is the first one I showed you, where you leave your character in the jaws of doom. Just shove Peter off that mountain, let him feel an awful air in his face, and put your period down.

End a chapter on a cliff-hanger. The reader is almost guaranteed to start your next one.

## The Mysterious Foreshadow

Now the ominous foreshadow. This is a *portent* of things to come; it's a promise to the reader that if he hangs on, excitement will come, the fearful confrontation will occur.

•• Foreshadows give a sense of something being just a little bit *wrong*, out-of-place, askew, or twisted.

Foreshadows can be omens, and anything can be an omen if you make something of it, although something a little different usually works best. You can use black crows, dark nights, cloud-streaked moons, moaning winds, broken sticks, cracks in china, storms, the day Friday the thirteenth, midnight, days when everything seems to go wrong that culminate in murder, a fortuneteller with one blind eye, a reflection in an antique-store mirror, shifting curtains, and keys that don't work.

But you can also make up your own omen, something fairly normal, and have it work maybe better than those other tried-and-true portents of disaster, at least in your particular mystery.

What makes an omen an omen is its coming before the sinister event; it's a *foreshadow*.

➡ If you want, a foreshadow can grow into the device upon which the plot turns.

Here's a simple example: A black high heel on a brand new shoe. First there is something different, maybe even *appealing* about the foreshadowing object, but the reader worries that perhaps the appeal is only an evil lure, and the reader is proved right.

The story opens with Juliette in a shoe store trying on different shoes and deciding on those high heels to please her mother, with whom she has to dine that night. You've got your omen working early on, and that's good. She'll pick the wrong heels, you see. She'll take the stiletto ones instead of the more sensible, stouter ones she prefers, and by so doing she'll get herself in a whole lot of trouble.

The next scene is Juliette's dinner with her mother, and afterwards Juliette is walking home. She's stomping along in her new black pumps. She's just had an argument with her mother who doesn't like the way Juliette dresses; Juliette's not chic enough. That's why, according to Mrs. Bestyet, her daughter got passed over for promotion in the advertising agency where she works, why her former boyfriend who's going to be a successful doctor gave her the go-by, and why Juliette wasn't asked to weekend at her best friend's new vacation ranch in Aspen, Colorado.

So Juliette is walking home after walking out on dinner with her mother, and she breaks the heel of her shoe. Well, it just seems to relate to what her mother has been badgering her about, and it makes Juliette want to cry. She doesn't mean to be a dump, she just doesn't think as much about clothes as her mother does. But she decides right then, bending to pick up the thin and stylish thing she can't even stand up in for one night without breaking, that she will become, before the next spring, a prize clotheshorse.

The heel has caught in the grid of a sewer grate. Stooping to pull it free, Juliette gasps in horror. A slimy long-fingered hand, clutching up from under the grate, has her heel and won't let go. (That's what caused it to

95

break, not Juliette's ineptitude.) "Help me," she hears, a heartbreaking, frail voice. Petrified, Juliette tries desperately to see just *what* is down there. She doesn't sense the man behind her, looking to other passersby as though he's trying to help. He leans over too and quickly injects the slender needle of a syringe into the back of Juliette's hair-swept neck. . . .

Okay. This story probably won't win an award. It's too grisly. But if you titled it "The Heel," you've gone from a foreshadowing omen to a plot-turning object and a play on words. Except that, to tell you the truth, this story *disturbs* me too much, so I'm going to ditch it and give you another example.

In my *Ice Fall*, a rich man on the *Titanic* hears a bell toll out at sea. He can't understand how; they're far from land and buoys. He shivers; he's been drinking and he sobers up a little. He hears the phantom bell again and hurries to his bed. Does this man survive the sinking? What do you think?

This foreshadowing omen not only got me nicely to the end of one scene, it set up a dramatic one to come, when the man doesn't survive the sinking.

- •◆ Try to get your omen to do a double duty, bring it back once in a while, make it count. They're great *intensifiers*.

In Daphne du Maurier's *The Birds*, the weather is the foreshadow and the omen. It's different. The cold comes in too quickly, too early for the season, and settles in and stays. There's something *wrong* this winter, and only the hero, at first, seems to notice. Soon everyone gets the idea, but by then it's too late. If you want to know how wrong things got, read the lady's story. It's one of the great ones.

- •◆ Foreshadows change the appearance of things. From something innocent, foreshadows give you *sinister*.
- •◆ Use foreshadows to strengthen your suspense, only not too much. Like salt, too much overpowers the mix. But with no foreshadowing, your mystery will be only fresh water when you want a surging sea.

# 11. LOVE 'EM OR LEAVE 'EM— SEX IN THE MYSTERY

I t used to be said that a subplot of love didn't belong in a mystery; it diluted the essence. This was said about westerns, too. You know, the cowboy kisses his horse or his gun and rides away with his buddy after shaking the woman's hand. She's left behind at the little white fence, a look of regret and wonder on her face. Wind from the horses' hooves (or something) lifts the folds of her long modest skirt. The sun sets on the end of a perfect day for him and, reader, forget about her. She's yesterday's news. The happy ending is all for him, he's shaken free.

The same kind of attitude flourished within the mystery. Mysteries were built on reason, on intellect, and love is only and all emotion. Never can the two co-exist, the wisdom ran, except in that man-despising subgenre, romantic suspense, which only shallow-minded females read.

That was the prevailing dogma, but it was never entirely true. No mystery stories are less sex-oriented that Conan Doyle's, yet even dear old inveterate bachelor Sherlock Holmes had his brush with love with Irene Adler, however lacklusterly it was displayed. And though Watson's marrying interfered with the time he was able to spend with his smart friend, Watson married nevertheless. And many of the problems Mr. Holmes had to solve had to do with helping lovers in their passionate and difficult intensities. So even the all-boy Holmes-and-Watson club, if it didn't admit women, did business with them every day. Indeed, they couldn't have gotten on without them. There'd have been too few mysteries to solve.

For sure, no world spins without love, and not many stories do either. The course of true love, legend has it, never does run straight. And along the twisty course is much good ground on which to build a mystery. Mysteries are also made upon the uneven ground of false love, or love grown old or cold, or love with the wrong man or woman.

In the golden oldie days of the grouchy private eye and the outraged tough-guy amateur, women were seen as the hero's "buddies" in skirts, or as dolls, meaning they had to be rescued, or molls, meaning they were more dangerous than male criminals because they didn't fight fair with their fists but won their battles with man-weakening allure. That's what *The Maltese Falcon* is all about, Sam Spade's love for a doll of a moll and how he beats it.

Still, there is this attitude. It still exists, and it's more right than wrong. What it's about, really, is the matter of proportion. In a conventional private-eye or puzzle mystery, or even in a cozy, the love interest should not intrude, override, or overwhelm the mystery's integrity. Love, which is feeling and emotion and other such mind deluding things, is not supposed to get in the way of the reasoning abilities of the hero or heroine who solves the mystery, unless the love contributes to the plot. The heart, in a mystery, is supposed to be subservient to the mind. Plot over feeling, that's the main thing. Okay, you can live with that. You can even use it to your purpose, as Dashiell Hammett did, and Daphne du Maurier, and almost all of us, every chance we have.

Nowadays it is fashionable to have a little interest in love and sex. It makes the hero or heroine more human, more contemporary and reasonable as a person, less a saint or superperson, less an ideal, a more well-rounded character. We're even getting away, these days, from masses of muscles, obligatory chase scenes, and twenty corpses to a book. These days we want our main characters to be like us, only a little better. Today's mystery heroes and heroines have trouble in their lives, and lacks and yearnings in their love lives, and they hate it, just like us.

- So, sure, have a love-to-come or a lost love burning, if you want to. You don't have to. Perhaps your plot won't support one; fine. But if it does, and you keep the love subplot in proportion, it won't hurt.
- Even a little sex won't hurt.

In a spy thriller, a lot of sex helps. James Bond without women would be like Nero Wolfe without his wine and orchids — not himself. In a great big "disaster" mystery, you might want all the sex you can think up just to grease the tangles in your many characters' lives. But in a normal genre mystery, a little sex will do. Use it to help define a hero's obsession with the mystery before him or her, or some such thing. And get the sexual draw to add to the suspense of the plot if you can. It needn't be hardcore explicit, though it could be, I guess. I leave that to your personal taste and talents.

●◆ Sex can play against the main plot or go with it.

In Scott Turow's *Presumed Innocent*, the sex takes place mostly in the main character's mind as he remembers his passionate moments with the murdered woman. In Dorothy Uhnak's *Victim*, the liberated sexual attitudes of the heroine are seen to be loose by some, and play an important part in the crimes of rape and murder with which the novel deals.

In *The Maltese Falcon*, Sam Spade's infatuation with the murderess causes Sam the main dilemma. In Mickey Spillane's *I, The Jury*, an evil beauty strips herself naked and tries to entice Mike Hammer into her arms so she can shoot him.

In most mysteries, the freer the sex, usually the more flawed the character, but this could be a dated attitude, changing even as you read this. Maybe you want to write a mystery about a woman who's trying to control her insatiable sexual appetite, and in so doing runs into murder and a life-threatening scenario. In solving the mystery, she solves her private problem too. I don't think I would write this one by choice, though I might, I might. I'd sure read it though. Real quick, you bet.

In a man's mystery, it is usually a woman who is sexually wicked. If she is beautiful, she might as well be, because the hero will think she is. In a mystery with a female hero, sometimes it's a man and sometimes another woman; in a "woman's mystery" it all depends.

●◆ But most of the time, in any mystery with women around, no one can be entirely sure of any one of them.

Even grandma has to be watched and little Baby Pinkums. By virtue of being female, they're suspect. There was Grandma Barker, remember, and *The Bad Seed* and *Lolita* are two good novels about "bad girls," both of them mysteries. And then women, even when they're innocent, often get the blame for what men do, or want to do, with them. Arthur Miller's drama, *The Crucible*, is an example of that.

●◆ Look, mystery writer, opportunities abound. Make use of them.

Women have always enjoyed a bad reputation. Eve seduced Adam, or so the story goes, and the world began to spin. But we ain't seen nothin' yet. Only now, as women's opportunities expand in the real world, will the mystery be able to really show off just how bad the female fair can be.

➥ And men as sex objects will come shortly into their own.

The charming wastrel. The suave con man. The seducer extraordinaire, the marry-er for money, the brute, the perverted creep, the pretty beach boy. Established gender roles are just waiting to be flopped. Do have a go. Write into your mystery the sex scene of your dreams.

➥ Just be sure it contributes to the plot. And keep a sense of proportion. After all, it is a mystery we're writing and so, in the final analysis, sex and love *are* less important than how you turn your screw.

And so is violence.

Television's "Columbo" is a lovable police detective, a harbinger of the new, more reasonable hero who sets a bad world right. Jessica Fletcher of "Murder, She Wrote" is his beneficiary. She's a mystery author in her sixties, and she's nice as pie. Both TV series characters were created by the great writing team of Bill Levenson and Richard Link. Both avoid violence. And after them will come, I predict, a *femme fatale* solver of mysteries. Glamorous or plain, she'll have a genius IQ and she'll be the biggest hit of all. Sherlock Holmes, meet your successor, Siren Suite. Maybe she'll be the grand old man's great-granddaughter or a distant cousin from a neglected family line. Or maybe she'll be nobody's daughter but her own, and she'll never have heard of 221B Baker Street.

And maybe you'll be her creator.

# 12. THE ROUSING CLIMAX AND THE DENOUEMENT

Everything is in place now for your finish. You've cleverly tangled your skein and sewn in all the complications so that solution, resolution, and happy ending look impossible. In fact, for your principal character doom impends; the villain seems to have won hands down, and for at least one other important character no sun shines.

But you know how, by pulling your vital string, the whole knot will slip loose into one long beautiful free line. What you want to know now is, how do you pull that string?

Let's say you're writing *Death on Smith Pond*. Miss Martha Smith, the little old lady villain, has lured Aurora Gorham, heroine, to the pond by calling her and telling her that her stepson, Gabriel, now out of the hospital, has come back to the pond and, crazily, she says, is stretched out on the now-frozen-over place where little Clemmy drowned.

It is late at night, and unusually warm for January. The surface of the ice is slick with a slight melting. Gabriel has confessed to being a drug seller for the drug dealer whose identity he still doesn't know, and he's been cooperating with the police in a setup to capture Rey Hermanas. Hermanas has learned of the setup and foxed it. But he was followed by Gabriel to his hut, and there Hermanas drugged Gabriel to insensibility and dragged him out onto the pond, cracked the ice around him and left him there to die. If Gabriel regains consciousness and, confused and not knowing where he is, tries to stand to get off the slick and weakened ice, he will break through.

To help this dastardly situation succeed, Martha Smith called Aurora, thinking that Aurora would go out on the ice after Gabriel and their combined weights would effect their double murder. Donovan Chance, although now quite attracted to Aurora, still thinks Aurora is the drug dealer of Land's Rest. He thinks she's trying to put the blame on her stepson and he means, for little Clemmy's sake, to see that Aurora doesn't get away with it. Watching Aurora's house from his—waiting for her to do something that will give her away—Don sees Aurora leave and follows her without her knowing. It is deep evening, a moonless night.

Rey Hermanas is in his hut, getting ready to leave town and Martha Smith; he's had enough. Martha has come down to the pond's edge to meet Aurora and show her Gabriel, sleeping out on the ice.

Aurora sees Gabriel and thinks only to save him. Trusting Miss Smith, Aurora slides out to Gabriel in her slip-on moccasins. Miss Smith chuckles to herself that Aurora is so unknowing she hasn't even brought a rope to attach to a tree to pull herself and her stepson back to land with. On her knees, Aurora wakes Gabriel from his drugged sleep; he comes to, thrashing and kicking and knocks Aurora down. The ice breaks, and in the dark of the moonless night Aurora and Gabriel plunge into black and deep and frigid water.

Don Chance, following along, sees Martha Smith at pond's edge, but misses seeing Aurora and Gabriel fall in. There's no sound of splashing. Both have sunk like stones, and it's so dark Don Chance does not even see that there's a new hole in the ice.

Miss Smith asks him to come into her house and have a cup of tea. She has something terrible to tell him about Aurora, something she found the day after his daughter drowned. It's been haunting her, she says, and she thinks he should know about it.

Don Chance turns away from the pond to follow the little old lady. In the pond, all is quiet.

So that's where you are. How do you set off the climax fireworks?

- ◆◆ Think of a string of firecrackers. Start with a little pop and then run up the line of bombs and rockets until you get to the last.
- ◆◆ Don't pussyfoot around now with atmospheric gush; atmosphere's of no use now. Dialogue that explains *anything* is only in the way. You can't break away from the scene because it's at its moment. If you cliff-hanger away now, you'll lose all the momentum you've been spiraling and twisting in, all the impact of the finale you've been building toward. In short, if you pull back now, you'll lose your juice.

➨ Start with a small pop, any little pop you can use to get the fuse ignited, and then run. Go right into your big scene and run it through to the end:

Giving his arm for Miss Smith to lean upon, turned away, moving up the flagstone path to Miss Smith's house, Don Chance hears water trickling, drop by drop, as though an icicle were melting on a porch eave. The spot on the ice where Gabriel's stuporous body lay has melted a slight depression. When Aurora and Gabriel fell in, this depression filled with water from the melting surface ice and is now dripping off, drop by drop, into the free water.

Don has brought a flashlight to help him in the dark. He pauses at the sound of dripping water. He turns and flashes his light. He sees the new hole in the pond and, white on white, Aurora's winter scarf, pulled off in her struggle and left behind on thin ice. And then in the beam he sees a disturbance in the hole.

"Get a rope," he tells Martha Smith and then he runs to the pond and sits down and begins to slide out to the middle. Aurora has Gabriel's head above water and is trying to lift him onto the ice and failing.

"Don't try to lift him, just hold him, I'm here," Don calls to Aurora. He lies down on his stomach to spread his weight and pulls himself toward her. The ice quivers as he comes.

And then Miss Smith, of course, does not fetch the rope but instead bursts in on Rey Hermanas who's packing to leave town. And Don Chance breaks away the rest of the weakened ice with his flashlight and then, where the ice is stronger, gets Gabriel out and then Aurora, who's exhausted and hypothermic but alive.

And then the detective, who was spying on Gabriel in the supermarket parking lot during the setup that didn't work, finally gets to the pond and helps Aurora and Gabriel to the hospital, and Miss Smith and Rey are stopped in their tracks, the cat food cans found full of cocaine.

Don Chance sits in the hospital waiting room for word of Aurora and Gabriel. While he waits, Rey Hermanas confesses everything down at the police station, and Miss Smith, unable to face public exposure of what she is, swallows a whole cat food can of cocaine and dies.

And then it is morning, and Don is admitted to Aurora's room; she and Gabriel will be fine. Miss Smith's will leaves her estate and Smith Pond to the town. Aurora and Gabriel and Don Chance walk out of the hospital holding hands on a clear mild morning which hints of spring. The end.

- ●◆ Once you get into the climax, run it through. Don't pause for breath or explanation, the explanation should all be there, obvious in the action. If it isn't try to get the explanation you need in a sentence or less—in a phrase—while the action careens around it.
- ●◆ And now you're done. After the climax and the *denouement*, your mystery is over.

The denouement is the "wrap-up," the tying up of the loose ends, the explanations of complications as needed.

But that old scene where the master-solver asks all the suspects to come into the library and then accuses one who turns out to be innocent in order to turn to the real murderer is very old hat, and we don't want to do it that way anymore unless we're writing a pastiche or parody. And you don't want to write that kind of mystery your first time out. Now you're learning how to write a real mystery, not a spoofing one.

So your denouement will have already been taken care of in your climax. Actions will explain, no fulsome explanations will be needed. Your mystery is over, virtue has triumphed, the wicked have been punished, life is back to normal. The end. Time to rewrite, smooth out, polish up, buff off and then prepare to submit and sell.

Congratulations.

Love it? So do I. I love to finish a book, finally finish it and send it all away. It only happens once or twice a year and it's better, all ways, than Christmas.

They say that Michelangelo hated to finish his sculptures; he left many of them still half-embedded in their stone. Psychologists talk about post-partum depression for the creative spirit after a work is done. Athletes talk about the letdown that comes after a major event is over, like a marathon or playing in the World Series.

I know what they mean. There has been such a psychic connection between your work and yourself. You have lived only to write this book, you have set up your whole life around it. Everything you think about is seen in terms of how it helps or hinders the completion of your task.

And then one day, early or late, it's over. You've pulled out the last extra adjective, you've changed your last pronoun, you've spun out the last magic and set your wand down.

Now, you ask yourself, what do you do? And what does it mean, after all, in the ceaseless roll of the world?

Well, this is what you do: Whoop a little. Have a sip of the bubbly or a hot fudge sundae. Go walk in the streets and feel the light on you, author of a completed mystery. Buy yourself something to commemorate the event. Take yourself to a movie, call a friend and brag.

➥ And then sit yourself back down. Now you've got to get your manuscript ready to go to market.

# 13. ABOUT TITLES

**B**y the way, have you titled your mystery yet? A good title is important. A good title helps sell your book. Everyone agrees to that. But what a good title is and how, exactly, it helps a work is not so easily determined, and no one I know seriously thinks a poor or ordinary title will sink a good book.

Although it might.

If it is true that word of mouth is the best advertising, and a new, ardent fan can't remember the name of your book to pass along his recommendation, my friend, you're in the soup. Forget about your name being remembered for a while. As a new author, unless there's a big, very big, publicity campaign attending your publication, or you're already famous for something else, for a long while the public won't even notice your name. Why should they? It's the read you're selling, not yourself. The public remembers book titles easier because book titles are named to be remembered and you probably weren't.

Still, new authors know instinctively that a good title helps sell a mystery because, before we were authors, we all bought one mystery and not another because we liked one's title better. Something about it piqued our interest or whetted our book-buying appetite and we bit. So titles are important. Try to find a good one.

When I spoke earlier about series characters, I mentioned titles you could have that connected the series in a reader's mind, like using the seven days of the week, or the list of deadly sins or commandments or some such universally known grouping, or the letters of the alphabet or, as John D. MacDonald did, a different color in each of his Travis McGees. Such ideas work and work well, the better as the series is established and the reader learns to recognize the latest as another in your series.

You can, for instance, team your hero or heroine's name with his or her latest outing, such as Greg Mcdonald does with his Fletch, or set up a title piece and then fill in the appropriate blanks as Erle Stanley Gardner did with his *The Case of the (Whatever)*, starring Perry Mason. Willard Huntington Wright, writing about Philo Vance under his pseudonym, S. S. Van Dine, titled his series, *The (Whichever) Murder Case*. Dick Francis, who doesn't like series characters so well, still uses short-word titles as one of his hallmarks. So there's *Dead Cert, Forfeit, Smokescreen* and such.

You do become known by what you do. It takes time, but a pattern eventually emerges, and then you have a kind of writer's "signature," something that identifies you in the book-buying public's mind. By the time you've written the ninth hour mystery of your projected twenty-four, people strolling by an aisle of new books will say, as they spot it, "Oh, here's (put your name here)'s latest. I have to get that!"

When I started, not having read this book of mine, I named my first novel the way I thought of it in my mind, *Sports Freak*. That was not so bad, but not so good either. I wouldn't put a work like "freak" in a title today. I find it off-putting. But that's what I did, and the book got noticed because it had a new and fresh background and I had a series going when I hadn't expected one, not being too bright in those days about such things. I had nowhere to take that first title, so I named the second in the series another cliché (the only association I could think of and I don't think anyone else picked up on it), *End of the Line* and the third and last of the T. T. Baldwin mysteries was titled *Hell Bent for Heaven*.

Well, I don't apologize. I rode the horse I'd saddled, and those first mysteries are dear to me. I wouldn't be the writer I am today without them.

But you be smarter.

- ◆◆ Give your title some thought. Plan ahead. There may be a series in front of you, so try to think of something that you can use as an identifying and connecting link.

Maybe you'll put "Night" in all your titles. Or a season. Or your character's name. My husband, Hillary Waugh, wrote a mystery with a Colonel Dagger as hero and I suggested the name *Dagger in Kenya*. "This way," I advised him, "you can have *Dagger in London, Dagger in Venice, Dagger in wherever we want to go.*"

Well, Hill's a nice man so he bought that, but his publishers didn't. They changed the title to *Murder on Safari* and it did very well, but he decided against a series based on his Colonel Dagger and maybe the name change had something to do with that.

And now about publishers changing your title.

They can do this, and sometimes they do. My *Turning Point* began life as *Whale's Turning*, the name of the Newport mansion where the romantic suspense takes place. Now I loved that title. I'd lived with it for a long time and it just thrilled me. But no, Worldwide Library said, your title will confuse. Readers won't know the kind of novel it is, they might think it's a nature romp or something equally misleading. And so *Turning Point* came out and sold in best-seller numbers, and that was that.

I could have pushed harder for *Whale's Turning* than I did. I didn't because I didn't know whether the publishers weren't right. I still don't. Who ever knows, once a decision has been made? *Turning Point* did well, and that was what we, author and publisher, both wanted. End of case.

Mary Higgins Clark's novel *Where Are the Children?* began life as *A Stranger Is Watching*. Mary liked the title, but it was changed, and as *Where Are the Children?* it was a hit. But still liking that title, Mary put it on the *succeeding* novel she wrote, and *A Stranger Is Watching* did well too. So the lesson here, I think, is that there's no perfect title for any one novel, although some seem to fit the work they hold wonderfully well.

Margaret Mitchell named her great novel *The Road to Tara* which nobody at Macmillan Publishing liked. Much like *Whale's Turning*, maybe it just didn't suggest what the book was about. Somebody there suggested the worse, *Another Day*, then *Tomorrow Is Another Day*, then *Tomorrow Will Be Fair*. Oh my, they were going, you see, from dull to yawn-yawn-yawn. Finally Miss Mitchell found *Gone with the Wind* and at the last moment changed her heroine's name from Pansy to Scarlett. Today, this title seems the only possible one for the Great American Novel, but at the time, close up, everyone involved was only trying to do the best he could.

So. Give yourself something to build on with your title. You want it, of course, to represent your mystery well, but you're also sowing seeds with this title for more of you to come. From the very beginning, from your first mystery-to-sell, think "career"; think: "What can I do with this title to help readers remember *me*?"

A last word on this. I originally wanted to title this work, *How to Write a Mystery and Survive to Write Another*. I liked that title. It was peppy and had a little sense of humor in the pun "survive," and it told, to my mind, what my intention of this work would be. But Writer's Digest Books had a series going of its own, into which it wanted my work to fit. The series would have similar covers that linked them; the series would have similar names distinguishable by the kind of novel writing (westerns, romances, mysteries) each work would cover. As one of a series on genre-writing, each would be easier to advertise and would, hopefully, sell better than if marketed alone. That sounded good to me, and so my title was preempted for the publisher's marketing ideas.

This happens sometimes and it is perfectly all right. It means the publishers are interested in helping you sell your book and, sir or madam, that happy situation is what all authors are after all the time.

- So think about your title, try to give it originality and a possibility of association with your next and the next after that. But don't think it's the only title possible or even the only good one. As Mr. Shakespeare said, a rose by any other name would smell as sweet. And your mystery, under many names, will read as well.
- Be prepared to give up your title graciously if a better one comes along or there's a compelling reason to do so, a reason which benefits your work, your publisher, and yourself.
- Mystery writing is a business. It's a little less than art and a little more than craft, but more than anything, it's a business. A title is, by its essence, an identifying mark, a selling tool. It may be more, but that's its heart.

Another last word. When you're translated into different languages or even published in different English-speaking countries, your titles will be changed.

- Please remember this: Only amateurs and gods write their words in concrete.

# 14. THE DISCIPLINE OF A WRITER'S LIFE

This year (so far) I've given up the chance to go to London. I said "no" to the biggest party of the year. Instead of seeing a friend's new film in premiere, I stayed home. I haven't done my running in a month. I live on the shoreline of Long Island Sound and not only do I not have a sportfishing boat, I don't even have a summer tan.

Why?

The answer is easy. I have a book to write. Two books if you want to know the truth, this one and a 400-page novel of suspense. And not just two books, but the best books of their kind of which I am capable. One is due in August and the second in October. Those opportunities in the first paragraph drifted in some months before the work in question was due, and neither book was finished. So I stayed home because *I had work to do.* There were specific scenes to be thought out, pages to rewrite, and (hardest, but we'll come to this) new pages yet to be written. So I stayed at my desk and did a day's work instead, and then at night, worn out, I thought about the next day's effort. Almost every day I could have been doing something else, but I didn't.

I'm a professional working writer and first things come first. If there's time left after the work is done, and I have an opportunity to play and enough joy in my step, then I'll do it. But as you become a writer you may find you just require long stretches of time in which, to the outside world, you seem to be doing nothing. You need time and solitude to sink down into the world you're creating in order to do your best work any one day.

•• Each day, your writing work comes first.

Let's talk about what this means.

It doesn't mean you'll never get out of your house again. You might very well jet off to Spain because you need to research that country for background. You might go to the party I excused myself from because you need new material for a weekend summer fete for the murder you're plotting out. You might trip along to the new movie or to the corner saloon because your work requires it. But if your day's work is waiting at your desk, you're going to be in more than you're out. And this doesn't mean you're going to become boring and slovenly. You'll be intensely more interesting and interested. Just wait; you'll see. Everybody loves a writer; strangers will tell you astonishing stories on the slightest acquaintance, and you'll be looking for fuel for your furnace. Whether it's the perfect plot that's revealed to you in a Main Street coffee shop by a shabbily dressed stranger who just happens to sit down beside you though all the other stools are empty, or only an interesting mannerism in a flirt you'll never see again after a shared moment over the canapés at a friend's bungalow, you'll find you notice more, remember more, see more around you. There's an old saw that says that everybody has a story, and that's true. But this is true too: You can make up your own story about anybody you want to.

Once I asked a druggist whom I exchanged pleasantries with, both of us sitting in the lounge of the National Press Club waiting for friends, for an in-every-household, undetectable-after-death, easy-to-carry-around-with-you-and-then-get-rid-of poison which hadn't already been worked to death by other mystery writers, and just like that, he gave me one. It appears to lethal effect in my *The Fortune-Hunters*.

Mystery writer Thomas (*Who Killed the Robins Family?*) Chastain tells of being stuck once in the middle of a mystery looking for the right face and mien of his villain. He just couldn't see him properly and it was stopping his work. For two weeks it had been driving him crazy. So he went out walking the streets, the way writers do sometimes, and he sat down in a restaurant for a bite to keep him going. And there he saw his villain, seemingly heaven sent, all by himself two tables away, wrapped around a three-tier bacon and chicken on rye. The man was just what Tom wanted, down to his hat. So Tom, seemingly staring into the space ahead of him, drank in the man during the time it took to eat his sandwich and then went back to his working place, and the writing flowed.

So, yes, your life will change. You're going to go from someone who wants to write a mystery to someone who is writing one to someone who has a manuscript to sell to someone with a book in the stores. And you will never be the same. I'm not talking about success and fame and hotpants fans now. I'm talking identity and how you look at the world. I mean, going to the grocery store will become something that has to be worked in. It can become a big pain, because it takes away from your writing time. Or it can be an opportunity, a background to be researched, a pool of people to scrutinize out of the corner of your eye. There is poison on those aisle shelves and plots in the cake mixes, and murderers every day stand in line.

You are going to change your identity as you write your novel. From wish to achievement, from longing to *fait accompli*, the "you" before will be forever metamorphosed into the "you" beyond.

Maybe by now you've got down on paper some of the particularities about yourself and the kind of mystery you're going to write, its setting perhaps, and its plot situation, but you haven't got a title yet, and you haven't written the first word. Or maybe you've already written a hundred pages and you're in a tangle. But before you get on to those things, you're going to do some serious thinking about the writer's life.

Look at your life now. Think a week through. And block out in it a certain segment of time, five days out of seven, which will belong to your novel from right this minute until the novel is done. Let's give it a year. Can you think up a working title, a "handle" for your novel? A title helps particularize it in your mind, helps give it definition. If you're not ready to title it, then call it whatever your idea is. Say, *Whatever Happened to Poor Tom?* and we don't mean Chastain, who does just fine.

Mary Higgins Clark, before she broke into the big time with her suspense novel, *Where Are the Children?*, wrote at her kitchen table early in the morning before she went off to her regular work. I call it her "regular work" because it was the work that was bringing home the pasta primavera and the vino. Soon, her "regular work" was novel writing, as may yours be. But before that happy day when Mrs. Clark realized her beans would come, henceforth, from fiction writing, she worked inconveniently and in short spates in the little time she could give to it. Here's the point: She squeezed out that time regularly, five days a week or maybe six, and maybe she got in a few extra hours on Sunday afternoon. She did this uphill slog for a year or two or three or four, come children's illnesses (she had five, four girls and one boy), come blind-date nights (she was a widow), come colds and tiredness and no one to tell her, "Hey, this is great." Finally, her first work completed and sold, it died on publication, and she went back to her kitchen table and started all over again. And that time, good for Mary, her novel went over the moon. For most of us, however, the leap into the best-seller ranks takes longer.

- So block out your time. You're going to need all of it you can get.
- Today, right now, take your notebook and look at your life and see where there's room for you to write each day, five days a week, until your first mystery is done.

This little act has just made you a writer. You're a practicing writer now. You're at it day by day.

- Don't worry about perfection.

Nobody's perfect. Even William Shakespeare, if he'd had the time, could have made his work better. In *Coriolanus*, for instance — do I dare? — Mr. Shakespeare talks too much. Some of his characters get just too windy, saying one thing several ways, probably as the thoughts fell out of his fingers. But as it is, it's been good enough for a long, long time. So nobody's perfect. Queen Guinevere, infatuated with Lancelot, said of her good husband, King Arthur, "All's wrong with perfection!" I think she meant that perfection was impossible to live with. And so we, happily, will not worry about perfection, though we will strive mightily to be *good enough*.

The caution I want to emphasize here is that a new writer's sense of inadequacy can sometimes stop him, can freeze the flow of the thought, and even dry up the idea. I remember one day I took six hours to get a single paragraph right. Finally I was satisfied. I had a beautiful paragraph, just what I wanted. And that was in the days when, though I was selling, I was still doing pieces for free and, yes, that paragraph was free, but never mind, I liked that paragraph and I liked finally getting it right. And here's my out on that: I had those six hours to give. My piece got done in time, as I knew it would. I was pacing within myself on that piece; I had the leisure to give six hours to that paragraph. You don't. Not now. Now you've got a mystery novel to write in one year, and only so many hours a day to put in on it, and you don't know how hard tomorrow's work is going to be, so you've got to push ahead now and come back later.

So you can't find the exact adjective you want to describe the suspect's manner, first time through. *Devious* won't do because the narrator isn't sure whether or not the suspect is telling the truth. *Sly* won't fit. *Uncooperative* is dull. This suspect is not trying to wiggle out, he's denying knowing anything at all about it. *Frightened*? God, no. You used that already about suspects one and two. What's the word you want; does the right one even exist?. . . .

&#x2023; Let it be.

Leave a hole in your sentence and go on, or type an underline under six or seven blank spaces and zip right by. The word will come to you. Rereading, you'll find it. Or just before you fall asleep at night. Or you'll be watching "Columbo" reruns and the phone interrupts and you'll say, as you stretch to answer it: "Obstinate! That's what the chef was being with the police sergeant! He wasn't going to tell about his passion for the singer no matter how hard the sergeant leaned on him, and he sure wasn't going to admit he'd slipped her the shrimp cocktail the nightclub owner said she couldn't have unless she paid for—That's what I was after!"

Okay. You're going to write two hours a day, five days a week. Now how do you figure that, translate that, into pages? Let's say a thousand words a day. Four pages. Does that seem a bit high for just starting out? Okay, seven hundred and fifty words. Three pages.

That's fifteen pages a week, sixty pages for the month. Let's lop off ten pages because of rewriting. That makes your quota fifty pages a month. The average length of a mystery novel is 60,000-65,000 words, yes? Splitting the average to 62,500 words gives us, at (rough count) 250 words a page, 205 pages. Sure, some pages will be less. Others will be more, don't worry about that. So you're going to write a novel of between 200 and 225 pages in manuscript. At fifty pages a month, you'll be typing *The End* four and a half months from now. But you've already given yourself an outside limit of a year. Even slipping a little, and we all slip sometimes, you're going to make it. It takes me about eight and a half months. Somehow.

The *concept* behind all this figuring is this: You make your workaday goal achievable, realistic. And then you give yourself room to fall off the mark and still stay on top of the whole thing. This way you won't lose heart the first time through. When life interrupts your best-laid plans as life inevitably does, you've built in for yourself a little slide, figured it in so that, even if you skip today, there's tomorrow. After all, you only have

114

to work five days out of seven. And even if you dip below your fifteen pages for the week, you only have to really get to fifty by the end of the month, so it will all average out. And even if you don't quite manage fifty pages every month, at the end of eight and a half of them, you still have three and a half more to bring your book in on schedule. See what I mean? No matter what, if you keep pegging away according to your *daily* timetable, you're going to finish your first mystery novel like a pro: You're going to finish up, slick and sweet, within your deadline.

And another thing: Don't trust your fledgling work to friend or foe until it is ready to be judged, and even then exercise cold reason and caution. Don't let your husband, your girlfriend, your drinking buddy, or your partner on your job take a whack at reading your manuscript while you're struggling through. Don't call your cousin who once published a poem in *Good Housekeeping*, don't send a Xeroxed copy to your long-lost buddy who was editor of the high school yearbook. Find a professional to evaluate your work. This professional is not the neighbor above you in Four-B with the great library, unless she happens to be a literary agent too, or an acquiring editor of a reputable publishing house.

When you've published, send all these other folks a postcard telling them where, if they like, they can buy a copy. Believe me, they'll enjoy your mystery much more that way, and so will you. Paying for something establishes that it has value.

On the other hand, one knowledgeable expert is not enough. One agent's kiss-off is another's rising star. One publishing house's dropped author is another's best seller. Don't put all your faith in any one opinion, even a laudatory one.

All right, if you have the ear of the editors at Random House, Crown, or Simon & Schuster, and one agrees to read your manuscript and then calls you next day and offers a contract, all right. Don't quibble. Just take it.

But let's say you don't. Let's say you know no one in publishing or in television or the movies. Do not worry, the universe unfolds as it should. Work on. When you're finished and your mystery is as good as you can get it, you'll find editors and agents willing to take a look at your work. Until then, as much as you can, keep your novel to yourself.

●◆ Secrecy heightens a mystery.

# 15. TO MARKET, TO MARKET

**O**kay, now comes the dog work, what my tennis teacher calls the "follow-through."

Dog work is not as hard as creative work, but it's duller. Dog work is work that won't make you better once you've done it, it just keeps you even. Dog work is work that has to be done so you can live, like laundering your shirts and taking your suits to the dry cleaners and brushing your teeth and making the bed and remembering to buy enough cottage cheese or gin or whatever it is it takes to get you through the coming weekend.

Some writers do not like the dog work concerned with getting their manuscripts ready to be seen and bought. I love mine. Why? Because it means I've got another little gem to sell. It means I've done it, I've climbed the mountain again, climbed it better this time, and now all I've got to do is clean up and then I can go play.

And I use my dog work to get a sense of the work as a whole, to see where I hit a new high or where I fell down and where I must do better next time. In one way the dog work is relaxing and in another it teaches one a huge humility. Beginning a mystery is for me the most wonderful time. I've struggled through the outline, defined my characters, I shiver in anticipating the great scenes waiting in that book for me to write. A new mystery is a new creation, unsullied as of yet, and perfect in my conception. It's a serious commitment of a year of my life. It's like creating the world.

After the world is made, I'm tired. I've beat my brains and patched and repaired and finally stood away somewhat older, somewhat wiser, and what's done is not the perfect child I meant to make. I may have done well here with my intention and not so well there. Here my foot slipped a little.

Here I slithered over a difficulty. Here I hit a new high. But the work is done and as good as it's going to get. Hurray, I say, it's time for the dog work.

- Somerset Maugham said, "No one writes as well as he would like to; he only writes as well as he can."

If, in the time of the dog work I can say that to myself, that I have written at the top of my ability that time through, then the dog work is good. It teaches me how to get better the next time. It shows me my strengths and my weaknesses. It gives me ideas for new mysteries, better characters, more clever surprises.

Dog work is dull but it rejuvenates. Dog work is happy because in doing it, you dream. As you dress your mystery for its meeting with your agent or editor or that first public buyer, you bless it and wish it well, and in some way, it blesses you back.

- So be happy with your dog work if you can. It's a healing time, a fun time. It's the time your addition to the world gets ready to take its place in its society.

Now that I've rhapsodized, just what is the dog work?
- Dog work is the final polish after the final rewrite.
- Dog work is saying "finished" to your mystery. Any more trying to make it better will only make it worse. It's admitting your work, this time through, is done.

It's the checking of spelling and commas, in or out, and the correcting of unintentional grammar mistakes. It's watching for an omitted word or a wrong one, one last time. It's holding the whole novel in your mind as a reader as you read it through in its entirety.

It's, oh my, getting *tired* of the thing.
- Dog work is the final printout after the final rewrite. One copy for you, and as many other copies as you mean to send out.
- It's getting each copy ready to be mailed, along with its cover letter.
- It's saying goodbye to one mystery and psychologically readying yourself for the next.

There are good books that show you how to prepare a manuscript for submission, and one of them is Writer's Digest Books' own *Guide to Manuscript Formats* by Dian Buchman and Seli Groves. This guide covers everything from letters to proposals to TV scripts, and I recommend it. But if all you need to know is how to get your mystery novel ready to go visiting, I can tell you simply.

Use clean white paper, 8½ x 11", 16 or 20 weight. Type your manuscript with black ribbon, or print it out on a letter-quality printer. Crisp and clear and dark is what you want; clean, sharp pages. Double-space, 24 or 25 lines to a page, one side of the paper only. Your name, then a slash and the title of the work are in the upper left-hand corner, the page number is in the upper right. That's about all that's really needed. Start a fresh page for each chapter and head up that page with its appropriate chapter number. Your title page is separate, and your dedication page. On your title page you name yourself as the author.

If you're agented, you don't put your address on the title page, the agent will stamp in his or hers or put on a sticker or something to identify the agenting company. So if you want an agent to represent you, don't put your address on the title page, just the title, then doubled-spaced under that and centered, 'By,' and then double-spaced under that and centered, your name.

If you're submitting on your own, of course type in the lower left-hand corner your address and telephone number.

## Proposals

If you haven't written a mystery yet, you might be wondering if it's a good idea to submit a proposal first, instead of a full manuscript. A proposal is the presentation of an idea of a book you intend to write.

> A proposal is a sales tool, much like a brochure put out by a magazine that wants you to subscribe. A proposal has to dance and leap and dazzle. An editor's mouth ought to water as he reads it. His fingers should just itch wanting to call your agent on the phone. Proposals are tricky. They're not novels, they're not working outlines. They're sales campaigns.

If you have not yet published a novel, I advise against a proposal. Most editors will be reluctant to write a contract on the strength of one, unsure you can carry off the projected full-length work. This first time around, write your novel and try to sell it whole. Next time, you'll have a mystery to show. Next time, you'll write a proposal.

But a word on that. Some writers don't like proposals. They think, and they're right, that to sculpt a good one takes considerable time. They think, and they're right about this, too, more often than not, that a novel sold from a proposal sells for less than the completed novel would. With a finished novel, your agent can take your manuscript to auction. With a proposal that's much less likely unless you're a "brand name." And if you are a brand name, you've got a publishing house already. Unless you want to change your publisher, you'll probably talk over your next project with your editor and not need a really fine proposal; he or she will accept your working outline, and you're off.

If you want more money next time out than your publisher wants to advance you, you might want to spiff up your proposal and have your agent send it out to different houses to gauge their interest. If you want to change houses, then a proposal can help you do that, too. And if, after establishing yourself, you want to break out of category, a really good proposal is the tool to use.

## Literary Agents

Now about agents.

If you're a nobody in the literary world and you know nobody in the publishing world, you can probably sell your first novel yourself in the time it would take you to get an agent. And if you're a know-nothing (as I was with my first novel to sell), you won't know one agent from another, and agents are like candy bars — some are better than others and some are better to one writer than to another.

And here's something to think about: When you get an agent, if the liaison doesn't sing, untangling your affairs from him or her once you have business going can be sticky.

My advice on agents is to go slowly. Probably your first novel won't get into big money, at least before publication. It is more important to be published your first time out than to try to make a fortune. If your novel goes, you'll get the money at the back, after publication. That's not so bad.

Wait a while before panting after agents. An agent works with what he has, and a known author with a track record is more attractive to an agent than an unknown, beginning one. Wait. Sell yourself for a time. Make a few contacts on your own. Take what you're offered and learn the track the first time around. This way, when you do join yourself to an agent you'll know better what to expect for his efforts on your behalf and you'll be better able to judge the job your agent is doing for you.

•• For this too is true: An agent works for you, not the other way around.

First-time authors are intimidated by agents, and that's no way for a writer to do business.

Almost all writers have agent horror stories. I'll tell you a few of mine.

I sold my first novel, the mystery *Sports Freak*, without an agent to St. Martin's Press. I sold it unagented because I could not find an agent to represent me. Inexpertly, I tried. I shipped *Sports Freak* away to three agents I'd read about in the book pages of the *New York Times*. They all said, after I wrote them about my novel, that they'd be glad to see it. My manuscript received, each was, to varying degrees, kind. One said that if and when I sold it myself, he would be glad to help out on the contract. I crossed that darling off my list right away. A famous woman agent said she couldn't sell me. "You have no name yet," she said, "and your novel has no sex." So she crossed me off straightaway. The third said, half-heartedly, she'd try. But when I called six months later to see how things were going, she didn't remember me or my manuscript and asked me to send her, post haste, another copy. So I crossed her off my list and went to the bibles of book publishing, Writer's Digest Books' *Novel and Short Story Writer's Market* and their *Writer's Market*, and R. R. Bowker Company's *The Literary Marketplace* which lists book publishers, what kinds of books they sell, the editor-head of each division, and addresses and telephone numbers. I made a list from that book of twelve hardback publishers of mystery novels, beginning with the house that published the most mysteries and working my way down.

First on the list, in those days, was Doubleday, where my writing course teacher labored. They turned me down very quickly, with no apology or explanation. Next was Simon & Schuster. There, after some months, a very nice editor invited me in, bought me a drink in a trendy publisher's-hangout pub, and turned me down. Regretfully, he said. (But they all say that.) Third was St. Martin's who, after four or five months of me barely breathing, bought. They offered me $3,000 and I took it. They mailed the contract. I thought I should get myself an agent then, and tried to, but again I had no success. Ten percent of three thousand dollars, it seemed, excited no agent I could find. So, tremblingly, I signed.

A year later I was published and I had a *success d'estime*. Critics raved in New York, Paris, and London. A movie producer took an option. I thought I was on my way. I wrote to three famous agents. They'll all want me now, I exulted. But they didn't. One, with a great big agency, passed me along to a junior agent just building her stable. One told me, after reading my praised novel, that he didn't like my work. And one, charming and slick, his name set in large gold letters on his door, said he would take me. I was so grateful I skipped all the way home from his office near publisher's row to my little basement studio where genius had triumphed.

But then the fine and winsome agent could not sell me. "I don't understand it," he said, "maybe you don't have it in you."

So I sold myself, again, to St. Martin's and wondered how the great world spun that I couldn't get on in it. Finally, when I had to sell myself a third time because the agent couldn't sell my big proposals, he called me up and dropped me. "You can't bring it in," he said. "I'm sorry but I can't handle writers who don't sell."

Well, that is one way the world turns. Toughen up or drop off, I told myself, and I toughened up.

So there's an agent story for you, one of the truths of the real world out there. Now let me say that the agent who dropped me is a good agent, a successful agent, and a good man. But he was a businessman and I was making him no money so he could not afford to give me his time. Yes, he might have been kinder, but that's no great matter. What matters, ultimately, is that he told me the truth. Feeling the way he did about me, I wouldn't want his representation. He'd take "no" for an answer too quickly, he'd stop trying to sell me too soon, or he'd sell me for a dollar when twenty might be made. No, that agent did me a true kindness and I'm glad he let me go. My god, what if he'd kept me and I never sold again?

That experience did not sour me on agents. That time of learning helped make a professional of me, and helped me to learn how, when the ball was in my court, to survive on my own. And writers need to know that. To end my agent story, let me just tell you that I now have a very kind one,

one my work excites, one who wants to see me do well, and one who sells me hard.

What I'd like you to know is this: Don't expect too much of anyone, and expect the most from yourself. After all, it's your career, your work. No one else's. None of us is perfect all the time. Agents, like writers, do the best they can with what they have. My best agent may be poison to you, and vice versa. That's just the way things are. Realize that, and still go out and try to find an agent, but take your time.

- ◆ You don't need an agent the first time out. And you may be better off without one until you're two or three mysteries down the road.

If you're selling, you can always find an agent. But again, if you're selling, for a while you won't need to. If you want a contract looked at, sure, get an agent or a literary lawyer. But don't expect an agent to find you the big deal or the big money before you've earned it. Money comes as you go. With success come the swag and the wine, and you may be a long time working in the vineyard.

If you like the vineyard you're in, if you want to stay there even when the crop is spare season after season, you'll turn out all right. One year, the harvest will be bountiful. And maybe then for years after. What is it, seven years for an apple tree to bear first fruit?

- ◆ It is not true that no one but a blockhead writes for anything but money. Money is the marker, the scale of your worldly success, nothing more. It is not the joy. It is not the inner sense of peace that comes from doing what you want to do the best you can.

If it happens that you and your agent fall out, for any of a hundred incompatible reasons, kiss the work you and he or she contracted together goodbye. Your new agent will not have anything to do with any of it. Your new agent will want to start fresh. So if you have work in print with one agent, you will have commerce with your ex-agent as long as those works are in print and paying royalties under that agent's contract. And until you get back your rights to sell the work again, after it has been out of print a certain number of years, that work will die on the vine because your ex-agent won't attempt to sell you any more, and your new agent will not want to get involved in work he did not initially represent.

•◆ Yes, writing is a business.

So while you're crawling toward an agent, you are going to try to sell your mystery on your own.

## Submitting Your Manuscript

First you'll write a one or one-and-a-half page cover letter telling who you are, the title of your mystery, and what the mystery is about. Then you will ask the editor to whom you're writing if he or she would like to see that mystery with intent to publish.

You can write to publishing houses whose addresses you can find in the writer's reference books I mentioned earlier, which list what editors head what trade divisions, and ask about their prospective mystery lines. When you hear, write the person who replies about your mystery.

Don't neglect the paperback houses. They're as big players these days as the hardcover houses, and in some instances, bigger. If the houses have mystery lines, they may send you guidelines and they may not. Mysteries are "freer" than category romances; a writer is more on his own to do the kind of mystery he likes.

•◆ Today the mystery is thriving, and it's an open market. If your mystery is a good one, it will sell and maybe quicker than you think right now. I hope so. I want your mystery to be good because I like to read a good one and I'm hoping for your success.

All right, on. Now you've sent your manuscript to three editors who have asked to see your work.

### Multiple Submissions

The question of multiple submissions is still an unresolved one. On the editors' side, they don't like them. After all, why should they? An editor is a professional, too, with a living to make, and if an editor likes a work, he or she doesn't want to have to fight for every one, and especially, maybe, doesn't want to have to fight for the new talent that's just been uncovered. As you rise in author recognition, multiple submissions may be resented less by an editor as part of the necessary evil of doing business in today's competitive markets, but even then editors try to avoid them. If an editor wants to keep his author, generally he'll try to treat the author well, because a well-treated author tends to stay, and grow from book to book with the same house. A trust becomes established and a friendship, and that's the best situation.

But from the new writer's point of view, single submission can be painfully slow. Remember when it seemed as though Christmas would never come? Well, that's how you'll probably feel the first time you send out a completed mystery manuscript to see if it can fly. And, in truth, the process is slow. Editors have a lot of work to do not reading, and so must read when they can, which often means at home nights and on weekends. And then an editor usually wants support in-house for the fledgling writer's manuscript, so another editor may read it when she can, and then a marketing person and maybe even a salesperson. And then there's usually a conference where editors pitch the books they like, and the budget is looked at. . . . The author is often the last to know.

So some authors, agented or not, send out multiple submissions. It is a courtesy to inform the editors you're contacting that you are not submitting only to him or her, but this is not always done because writers do not want to prejudice their case, and the less well known the author is, the more prejudice there may be.

My advice is to multiply submit and cross the dangerous bridge of what-do-I-do-when-two-editors-bite when you come to it. Most of the time, getting one house interested is a good accomplishment. Many truly outstanding manuscripts have drifted from house to house seeking a publisher before they were bought and acclaimed by the public. *Jonathan Livingston Seagull* is a famous example. *Lolita* is another. And the trouble James Joyce had publishing *Ulysses* is taught in many Lit 101 classes, or was when I went to school. So, being on the writer's side, I say maximize your options and submit to three houses at a time. Would I tell them I was multiply submitting? Not if I was submitting at mid-list level. (Mid-list is a euphemism for all books not expected to become best sellers.) If I was negotiating what my agent and I thought could be a major book, of course we'd tell all interested parties, and then we'd hold an auction. But trying to break in, I'd try to speed up the acceptance process any way I could.

## Following Up on Your Submission

Give the houses three months. During that time you're writing short stories maybe, or you've plotted out your second mystery and are, I hope, sailing right along with it. If you haven't heard any news, good or bad, from any editor after three months, one morning about ten, sit down by your telephone and call.

&bull;&bull; Do not write a follow-up letter. I'm sorry it is true, but letters today are stodgy and old-fashioned as far as asking about one's manuscript is concerned. Call your editor.

When you get her, tell her who you are and that you submitted *The First Mystery* and when, and does she have any news for you about it? She'll probably say she'll get back to you, take your number and out. But now you've made a personal contact. You talked together on the phone. You haven't met, but you know an editor already. Don't push for an answer and don't ask any questions other than the one I've given you. Just be pleasant, ring off, and let her ring you back. Go through the three houses that have your manuscript like this, and then get on with your day.

If an editor isn't in to take your call, leave your message nicely with her or his secretary. You know: "My name is ( _____ ), and I'm calling about my mystery, ( _____ ). I submitted it to ( name of editor without a Mr. or Ms. attached ) on ( date of submission ), and I'm wondering if a decision has been made." The secretary will take your number and the editor or the secretary will get back to you, either by letter or telephone, and that's all right. That's how it's done. It's simple, it's polite, it's business. And it works.

Okay, here's the worst scenario. All three houses turn you down. Move on to the next three until you've covered all the houses in America and Canada publishing mysteries that you can find. This, at three month intervals, should probably take you about a year and a half. By that time, you'll have finished your second mystery, won't you? And so now, since you know all those editors with whom you had prior dealings, you will write again, telling each about your new book and wondering if he or she would like to see that one. . . .

Maybe, also, in that time of waiting you joined a writer's group. You've met some published writers there and talked shop together and met an editor or two at a gathering or writer's conference or workshop, so you feel more a part of the writing community. You've learned, you're committed, you're just waiting out that first sale. Maybe you've sold a short story to one of the small mystery magazines, so you've now got a credit or two to add to your cover letter. And you've met an agent or two you like at the writer's group too. See how far you've come? Hang in, hang on, keep writing, keep getting better, keep trying.

And one day, bingo.

It'll probably happen just like that, too. One day you'll get a letter or a call saying, "Yes, we like your work here and we'll be sending along a contract. Welcome to the club."

Hot dog.

Don't let the fact that the contract isn't for a million dollars, or that your editor may want a bit of rewriting, or that your novel won't be out in the stores for another year and a half dim your splendor. You've won, and all glory to you. Savor your achievement. Don't start comparing yourself to somebody on the best-seller list. That's next year's battle, or the year after that. Enjoy your honeymoon. You've pulled your train—you thought you could—relax a moment and enjoy the view.

There's a lot more work ahead of you now that you're a real soon-to-be-published writer. You've become one of the lucky ones. You've become one of us.

One final thing. I'd like to hear from you, to know if this book of mine helped or if what you really wanted to know I didn't tell you. Maybe you'll send me a complimentary copy of your mystery once it's out? I'd very much appreciate that. I'd like to have a library shelf of mysteries I helped along, in however small a way.

Write to me in care of the Editorial Department, Writer's Digest Books, 1507 Dana Avenue, Cincinnati, Ohio 45207. I'll write back.

See you in the bookstores.

# Index

# OTHER BOOKS OF INTEREST

**Annual Market Books**
 Children's Writer's & Illustrator's Market, edited by Lisa Carpenter (paper) $17.95
 Guide to Literary Agents & Art/Photo Reps, edited by Robin Gee $15.95
 Humor & Cartoon Markets, edited by Bob Staake $18.95
 Novel & Short Story Writer's Market, edited by Robin Gee (paper) $19.95
 Photographer's Market, edited by Sam Marshall $21.95
 Poet's Market, by Judson Jerome $19.95
 Songwriter's Market, edited by Brian Rushing $19.95
 Writer's Market, edited by Mark Kissling $26.95

**General Writing Books**
 Beginning Writer's Answer Book, edited by Kirk Polking (paper) $13.95
 Discovering the Writer Within, by Bruce Ballenger & Barry Lane $17.95
 Freeing Your Creativity, by Marshall Cook $17.95
 Getting the Words Right: How to Rewrite, Edit and Revise, by Theodore A. Rees Cheney (paper) $12.95
 How to Write a Book Proposal, by Michael Larsen (paper) $11.95
 Knowing Where to Look: The Ultimate Guide to Research, by Lois Horowitz (paper) $18.95
 Make Your Words Work, by Gary Provost $17.95
 Pinckert's Practical Grammar, by Robert C. Pinckert (paper) $11.95
 12 Keys to Writing Books That Sell, by Kathleen Krull (paper) $12.95
 The 28 Biggest Writing Blunders, by William Noble $12.95
 The 29 Most Common Writing Mistakes & How to Avoid Them, by Judy Delton (paper) $9.95
 The Wordwatcher's Guide to Good Writing & Grammar, by Morton S. Freeman (paper) $15.95
 Word Processing Secrets for Writers, by Michael A. Banks & Ansen Dibell (paper) $14.95
 The Writer's Book of Checklists, by Scott Edelstein $16.95
 The Writer's Digest Guide to Manuscript Formats, by Buchman & Groves $18.95
 The Writer's Essential Desk Reference, edited by Glenda Neff $19.95

**Nonfiction Writing**
 Creative Conversations: The Writer's Guide to Conducting Interviews, by Michael Schumacher $16.95
 How to Do Leaflets, Newsletters, & Newspapers, by Nancy Brigham (paper) $14.95
 How to Sell Every Magazine Article You Write, by Lisa Collier Cool (paper) $11.95
 How to Write Irresistible Query Letters, by Lisa Collier Cool (paper) $10.95
 The Writer's Digest Handbook of Magazine Article Writing, edited by Jean M. Fredette (paper) $11.95

**Fiction Writing**
 The Art & Craft of Novel Writing, by Oakley Hall $17.95
 Characters & Viewpoint, by Orson Scott Card $13.95
 The Complete Guide to Writing Fiction, by Barnaby Conrad $18.95
 Cosmic Critiques: How & Why 10 Science Fiction Stories Work, edited by Asimov & Greenberg (paper) $12.95
 Creating Characters: How to Build Story People, by Dwight V. Swain $16.95
 Creating Short Fiction, by Damon Knight (paper) $11.95
 Dialogue, by Lewis Turco $13.95
 The Fiction Writer's Silent Partner, by Martin Roth $19.95
 Handbook of Short Story Writing: Vol. I, by Dickson and Smythe (paper) $12.95
 Handbook of Short Story Writing: Vol. II, edited by Jean Fredette (paper) $12.95
 How to Write & Sell Your First Novel, by Collier & Leighton (paper) $12.95
 Manuscript Submission, by Scott Edelstein $13.95
 Mastering Fiction Writing, by Kit Reed $18.95
 Plot, by Ansen Dibell $13.95
 Spider Spin Me a Web: Lawrence Block on Writing Fiction, by Lawrence Block $16.95
 Theme & Strategy, by Ronald B. Tobias $13.95
 The 38 Most Common Writing Mistakes, by Jack M. Bickham $12.95

Writer's Digest Handbook of Novel Writing, $18.95

Writing the Novel: From Plot to Print, by Lawrence Block (paper) $11.95

**Special Interest Writing Books**

Armed & Dangerous: A Writer's Guide to Weapons, by Michael Newton (paper) $14.95

The Children's Picture Book: How to Write It, How to Sell It, by Ellen E.M. Roberts (paper) $19.95

Comedy Writing Secrets, by Mel Helitzer (paper) $15.95

The Complete Book of Feature Writing, by Leonard Witt $18.95

Creating Poetry, by John Drury $18.95

Deadly Doses: A Writer's Guide to Poisons, by Serita Deborah Stevens with Anne Klarner (paper) $16.95

Editing Your Newsletter, by Mark Beach (paper) $18.50

Families Writing, by Peter Stillman (paper) $12.95

A Guide to Travel Writing & Photography, by Ann & Carl Purcell (paper) $22.95

Hillary Waugh's Guide to Mysteries & Mystery Writing, by Hillary Waugh $19.95

How to Pitch & Sell Your TV Script, by David Silver $17.95

How to Write & Sell Greeting Cards, Bumper Stickers, T-Shirts and Other Fun Stuff, by Molly Wigand (paper) 15.95

How to Write Horror Fiction, by William F. Nolan $15.95

How to Write Mysteries, by Shannon OCork $13.95

How to Write Romances, by Phyllis Taylor Pianka $15.95

How to Write Science Fiction & Fantasy, by Orson Scott Card $13.95

How to Write Tales of Horror, Fantasy & Science Fiction, edited by J.N. Williamson (paper) $12.95

How to Write the Story of Your Life, by Frank P. Thomas (paper) $11.95

The Magazine Article: How To Think It, Plan It, Write It, by Peter Jacobi $17.95

Mystery Writer's Handbook, by The Mystery Writers of America (paper) $11.95

The Poet's Handbook, by Judson Jerome (paper) $11.95

Powerful Business Writing, by Tom McKeown $12.95

Successful Scriptwriting, by Jurgen Wolff & Kerry Cox (paper) $14.95

The Writer's Complete Crime Reference Book, by Martin Roth $19.95

The Writer's Guide to Conquering the Magazine Market, by Connie Emerson $17.95

Writing for Children & Teenagers, 3rd Edition, by Lee Wyndham & Arnold Madison (paper) $12.95

Writing the Modern Mystery, by Barbara Norville (paper) $12.95

**The Writing Business**

A Beginner's Guide to Getting Published, edited by Kirk Polking (paper) $11.95

The Complete Guide to Self-Publishing, by Tom & Marilyn Ross (paper) $16.95

How You Can Make $25,000 a Year Writing, by Nancy Edmonds Hanson (paper) $14.95

This Business of Writing, by Gregg Levoy $19.95

Writing A to Z, edited by Kirk Polking $22.95

To order directly from the publisher, include $3.00 postage and handling for 1 book and $1.00 for each additional book. Allow 30 days for delivery.

Writer's Digest Books

1507 Dana Avenue, Cincinnati, Ohio 45207

Credit card orders call TOLL-FREE

1-800-289-0963

Prices subject to change without notice.

Write to this same address for information on *Writer's Digest* magazine, *Story* magazine, Writer's Digest Book Club, Writer's Digest School, and Writer's Digest Criticism Service.